Spring Clean
YOUR LIFE

TOOLS TO

TRANSFORM

YOUR SPACES

AND

YOUR SPIRIT

by GAYLAH BALTER

To Louise
Gaylah Balter

Cover photo from gettyimages.com
Cover and interior design by Kathy Campbell
Back cover photo by Alan King

ISBN+10: 0-9707861-2-3
ISBN+13: 978-0-9707861-2-8

Publisher's Cataloging-in-Publication Data
Balter, Gaylah.
      Spring clean your life-- : tools to transform your spaces and your spirit / by Gaylah Balter.
        p. cm.
      Includes bibliographical references and index.
      ISBN 0-9707861-2-3

      1. House cleaning. 2. Orderliness. 3. Conduct of life. I. Title.

     TX324.B35 2005   648'.5
                      QBI05-200171

Printed in the USA

Learning Tree Books
1605 Prospect Ave, NE
Olympia, WA 98506
email: gaylahbalter@earthlink.net
web: learningtreebooks.com

ACKNOWLEDGMENTS

This book was written and conceived when much of my energy was devoted to gaining my health back. Writing it helped me to focus on being positive, proactive, and patient.

My children, Anaya and Ariel provided support, ideas, and critiques that helped to gel my ideas and bring them to fruition. Along with their partners, Karen and Alan, they nurtured me in ways that I could only have dreamed were possible. I am today the person I have become (changed in many good ways) as a direct result of their efforts, care, and abiding love. They made this book possible.

I also wish to thank Jennifer Dotson for her thoughtful and expert editing. Her efforts helped to make the book easier to read, use, and understand. Kathy Campbell, my formatter and cover creator, contributed artistic, aesthetic, and practical ideas which completed the process of a beautiful presentation and improved readability.

In *Six Weeks to a Simple Lifestyle*,
Barbara De Grote-Sorensen remarks,
"I had trapped myself into a lifestyle that didn't
mirror my true values and priorities."

CONTENTS

LIVING WITH LESS CREATES SPACE FOR SPIRITUALITY
TO GROW AND FLOURISH IN YOUR LIFE.

THE GREAT THING ABOUT MATERIAL THINGS—
THOSE YOU HAVE AND THOSE YOU DON'T—IS THAT
THEY NEVER LIE ABOUT WHAT YOU'VE BEEN THINKING.

Anonymous

INTRODUCTION

Is it possible to create a life free of clutter, filled with balance and calm, and deliciously easy to maintain? Do I hear a lot of grumbling in the background? Is it because you have tried and failed at these tasks? Or is it because you don't know where to start? You may also feel overwhelmed or confused. Does your energy immediately go elsewhere whenever you start to think about the status of your "stuff"?

In my classes designed to help people clear their clutter, I have encountered all these responses from my students. You are part of a large group of people, growing larger each minute, who feel space challenged. The fact is, everyone has some clutter, even the most organized and neat person that you or I know. Clutter is part of living in the 21st century.

Be assured that cleaning is known to be one the best therapies for whatever ails you. Organized and neat people report that they keep at it daily. That is, they work on their spaces as part of daily living, and this helps keep the unending "stuff" under their control. We can learn from them.

This book will demystify the sources of the clutter in your life so it can stop limiting who you are, where you are going, and who you wish to become. You may be holding onto your clutter for many reasons. Sometimes you might not even remember why, and conveniently go on to something else. It is just too hard, too exhausting, too anxiety-producing to address. You are clearly overwhelmed.

I present many ideas and solutions about issues that you won't find in any other book about clutter or space clearing. I have researched psychological, social, and spiritual outcomes of junk in the home and workplace and incorporated my findings throughout this book. That is why I have included chapters on simple living choices, setting boundaries, and help for pack rats and procrastinators, as well as whole chapters on the mental, emotional, and spiritual forms of clutter and solutions for each of these. I stress often that positive thinking will lead to proactive thinking, which will in turn lead to trying out new ideas, behaviors, and actions that will recharge your batteries.

Throughout, I have tried to bring compassion, understanding, and empathy to my discourse and solutions to problems. I believe that people are in a lot of pain over their messes. Their homes don't reflect their true values and who they really are. I hear their despair with every class I teach and as I meet people who have read my first book, *Clean Your Clutter, Clear Your Life*.

I am honored to offer you tips, help, suggestions, ideas, and solutions for all aspects of your clutter issues. Good luck on your journey.

—GAYLAH BALTER, 2006

PART 1

THE
WHO, WHAT, WHY, WHERE, AND HOW
OF
CLUTTER

CHAPTER 1

Spring Clean Your Life

✓ QUIZ

1. Do you make to-do lists?

2. Do you value setting goals?

3. Have you noticed that piles of clutter attract dust & grime?

When you start your spring cleaning chores you are motivated and committed. You can use this same enthusiasm to spring clean your life! That amount of zeal and planning can create a system for keeping your home or office clutter-free all the time, effortlessly.

What does spring clean mean? It means cleaning up everything in sight after a winter's accumulation of dust and grime. It means creating sweet smelling spaces that offer a place to relax, work, eat, and dream. My students report back to me that cleaning up their space brings light into the home and makes them feel very good.

What does spring clean your life mean? It means eliminating the mental, emotional, and spiritual clutter in your life, which has increased the physical clutter in your environment.

Why do you need to spring clean your life? Mental clutter, emotional clutter, and spiritual clutter make clearing the physical clutter in your life more difficult. They keep you from thinking clearly about how to change and how to address your physical clutter. They drain your available energy, create barriers to resolving old issues that you have carried around with you for years, and prevent you from living the life you desire. Lastly, they sap your ability to establish an environment which fosters your soul's desires, values, and spiritual needs.

It is important to take responsibility for your cluttering ways. The truth is simple. You have clutter in your life because you have given more importance to other matters rather than taking care of your surroundings, your thoughts, and your behaviors. Cutting to the chase, your life has consisted of random decisions, a lack of conscious living, and stagnant blocked energy from all that "stuff." Since you don't know where to start or how to begin and are completely overwhelmed by the mess around you, the piles seem to grow and have taken over your spaces.

Honesty with yourself and your goals is one of the most im-

CLEARING CLUTTER IS ONE OF THE
BEST SELF-IMPROVEMENT STRATEGIES
YOU CAN USE TO JUMP-START YOUR LIFE.

portant things to consider. Are you living your life in accord with your goals, desires, and values? When you aren't, tension and anxiety take over. These can produce cluttering behaviors that manifest as physical, mental, emotional, and spiritual clutter. Establishing consistency between your inner and outer worlds will help resolve all forms of clutter, restore your personal power, and elevate your self-esteem.

Starting out to **Spring Clean Your Life** will require thought, planning, and effort. Please look over the following suggestions to help you on your way.

Look at your Space with New Eyes

1. Look around your space and pay particular attention to the areas in which you spend the most time. Your goal is to make these spaces contain things that make you feel good and contribute to your life in a positive way. Things that have sad or negative memories attached to them need to go.

2. Make sure that everything around you contributes to your health, well-being and growth.

3. As you change your environment on a physical level you will notice that this will change you emotionally and spiritually. Look into the chapters on clearing mental, emotional, and spiritual clutter to take you even further in achieving your goals.

"GOALS PUT YOU IN CONTROL. THEY PUT
YOU IN THE DRIVER'S SEAT OF YOUR LIFE.
GOALS ARE VERY POWERFUL."

DONNA WATSON, PHD

❧ TIP ❧

Write down three short-term and three long-term goals, a plan to implement them, and a way to maintain the results. Keep these in a journal that you can refer to in the future as a record of your progress, along with any other data you wish to include about your space-clearing journey.

Setting Goals

Goals enable you to unlock your potential.

Lists

Lists will help you achieve your goals. Lists help you keep track of your goals. Lists serve as powerful wish-fulfillment tools.

1. List three obtainable goals.

2. List obstacles to achieving these goals.

3. List people whose help and cooperation you need and others that you could call on for help.

4. List all the ways you will benefit from achieving your goals.

5. Think on paper. Write out every detail of the problem and then take the most logical step to solve it.

6. Set a deadline and write it on your calendar.

7. Make a plan to achieve your goals.

Make a list of every idea or insight
you can gain and have gained
from setbacks or difficulties.

Making lists is a very good habit to introduce into your life.

What Do Lists Do For You? They . . .

- Jog your memory
- Unclutter your mind
- Establish your priorities
- Keep you focused
- Keep you motivated
- Help you visualize
- Clarify your thoughts
- Help you set goals
- Satisfy you when you can cross off items*

One of the problems with our society is that we have not changed the learned response to scarcity. Putting aside and storing stuff for future times of need was wise and goes back to prehistoric efforts to deal with the environment. It served our forebears well over the years. Now we live in a different era where ease of buying is the norm. There is no scarcity or lack, yet we continue to stock up and store. Bulking up has also taken over our bodies as more of us put on weight. Might there be a subtle connection here?

* Source: Gloria Silverio, Life Coach, excerpted from *Delicious Living Magazine,* 2004.

Things To Think About

When you establish order in your environment
the following will undoubtedly take place in your life.

1. You can locate long lost items and prevent other items from getting lost.

2. You can get rid of your guilt and anxiety.

3. You can enjoy your family and your home more.

CHAPTER 2

Understanding Why You Clutter

✒ QUIZ

1. Is paperwork piled in stacks everywhere?

2. Are the contents of your closets a mystery?

3. Have you lost control over your time?

4. Has your collection of porcelain ducks, frogs, elephants, etc., lost the interest or enjoyment for you that they once had?

5. Do you frequent garage and yard sales and flea markets and don't know where to put all the stuff you bring home?

Why is it so important to understand why you clutter? The ability to understand how and why you clutter will help you understand the roots of your cluttering habits and behaviors and provide you with tools to take care of it. Clutterers tend to avoid looking at the causes of their clutter because they are so overwhelmed and stressed with it all.

We live in a society with constant messages to buy, to acquire, to collect, to own, and to desire more of everything. We are unable to stop. Shopping at flea markets, garage sales, yard sales, estate sales, second hand shops, malls, online auctions, and the internet is a national pastime. I could add trash day findings to the list. President Bush even made it a national priority when he asked Americans to shop to invigorate a lagging economy.

We bring our purchases home to our already overcrowded spaces. Passages are blocked, closet doors cannot be closed, piles of papers hide our desks from view, unopened mail covers the dining room table, and clothing lies strewn on the floors of every bedroom.

So much stuff around you creates stress and makes you feel that as an adult you are a failure. It keeps you tied to the past and makes it difficult to live in the present. Every task you attempt takes much longer than if your space was in order. The jumbled and chaotic nature of your surroundings creates an environment that fosters scattered thinking and poor decision making skills and becomes a constant source of irritation in your life.

If you had a genie that would grant you any wish, would you ask that all the clutter in your home disappear? If your answer is yes, you are not alone. Genies, unfortunately, are not readily available, so we are left with the job ourselves. You can do it and I'd like to help. It is possible to live a clutter-free life without a genie.

How Changing Your Self Talk Can Help With Your Clutter

Letting Go Is Good To Do

Letting go of old ideas, broken promises to yourself and others, and life choices that no longer serve you is an important part of solving your clutter puzzle. These mental, emotional, and spiritual forms of clutter make it more difficult for you to attend to your physical clutter. They increase your levels of anxiety and stress, lower your energy levels, and create barriers to any positive action.

In *Living The Simple Life* Elaine St. James says, "Getting rid of clutter is not about letting go of things that are meaningful to you, it's about letting go of the things that no longer contribute to your life so that you have the time and the energy and the space for the things that do." This is important to consider. In Chapter 15 you will find specific methods to help you with the difficult process of going over your stuff and eliminating items that you no longer love and those that are not contributing positively to your life anymore.

Some of the old ideas might be in the form of messages and tapes running in your head. It is time to re-examine them and determine if they are still needed. One way to **Spring Clean Your Life** would be to create new self-talk tapes, new habits, and new ways of thinking. You will find more on this in Chapters 3, 5, 6, and 7.

Here are some examples of these messages:

- It's a sin to throw anything away.

- I may use it someday.

- Aunt Velma gave it to me.

- It has been in my family for generations.

- Maybe the kids will want it?

- Waste not, want not.

- Did I get my money's worth?

Do these sound familiar? Most clutterers claim at least one of them. You may not even be aware of these messages because they lie below the conscious level of thinking. They are stored there and influence your actions. Be honest with yourself. Look at your old ways of thinking to determine if any are playing a role in why you keep so many possessions that you don't love or use.

Decisions Regarding Purchases

It is important to remember that you make the decisions about what to buy and bring into your home or office. Everything is there because of some decision you made. Take a good look at how and why you make purchases and also what items you have decided to keep.

TAKING A LOOK
AT YOUR SHOPPING PRACTICES:

- Use the thirty-day rule. Make a list of what you wish to purchase, post it, wait thirty days, and then revisit your list to see if you still desire each item.

- If you decide to purchase something, please make a commitment to get rid of something. Keep the energy flowing and your possessions in line.

- Shopping can sometimes fill a personal void. Examine this in your life.

- Don't forget that you have the burden of maintaining everything you bring into your space.

- Changing how and why you make purchases changes how you relate to the world.

- Try not to go shopping when you are feeling anxious, bored, have time on your hands, need entertainment, or want to be with friends. Browse and look for fun only.

Begin to take control of your buying, shopping, and accepting of gifts. Can't seem to say "no"? Here's some help: You can refuse to buy and/or accept new stuff into your life.

EVERYTHING YOU ARE OR WANT TO BE IS INFLUENCED
BY EVERYTHING AROUND YOU.

Five Ways to Tell People You Have to Refuse Their Gifts, Cast-Offs, and Offers:

1. Gosh, I would like to but I just don't have the space for it.

2. My partner would really object.

3. I've already got one just like it.

4. I have made a decision not to accept more things than I can take care of.

5. I really don't need another one of those.

Things To Think About:

1. Spring cleaning your life will not happen unless you address all the areas of clutter in your life.

2. It is important to try a few solutions at a time. Work with them and then go to others.

3. Be extremely patient with yourself and reward yourself for each success and improvement, no matter how small it may seem to you.

4. All forms of clutter in your life did not appear suddenly and will need some time to resolve.

CHAPTER 3

Getting to the Heart of Why You Clutter

✒ QUIZ

1. Is your house so messy you can't find a comfortable place to sit?

2. Do you spend hours looking for lost documents, bills, books, or eyeglasses?

3. Do newspapers and magazines pile up unread?

4. Do you often misplace keys, purses, gloves, or other items used on a daily basis?

5. Do you want to get organized but things are in such a mess you don't know where to start?

It is a good idea to look at your habits and ways of thinking and doing things. Why? Unless you change some of the habits and thought patterns that you have had for years, you won't be able to break through the feeling of being overwhelmed, embark on a project, and maintain the good that you have accomplished.

Healing Your Communications

Saying "No"

Another example of letting go of old ideas and life choices is the simple act of saying "no." When asked to do a job you don't have the time for or the desire to do, it is so much better to be honest and say "no" than it is to say "yes" as you might be in the habit of doing. When you are honest with yourself and others, your authentic self takes charge, your self-esteem improves, and you feel clear and in line with your innermost feelings and desires. When your communications and actions are in line with your wishes, much of the clutter in your mental and emotional life disappears. You cannot please everybody in spite of what your family of origin taught you.

Shoulding

I call living with broken promises "shoulding on yourself." We all do it. Shoulding is one of the ways that you store guilt and at the same time absolve yourself of responsibility. This can sabotage all the good work you have been doing for yourself.

It is good to experiment with eliminating should, have to, and must from your speech. Using these words sounds like someone is making you do something. Try substituting choose, wish, or desire into your speech pattern. Using more positive words will elevate your level of communication and feed your psyche with new patterns of thinking and speaking. Words have the power to change your thoughts and feelings and provide you with reinforcement for the changes you are making in your life.

Try the following positive phrases to help you get on your new path.

"I now choose for myself . . . ."

"I believe that everything happens for a purpose . . . ."

"I am free of guilt related to my clutter, and I have started to . . . ."

Author Donna Watson, PhD, in her book *101 Simple Ways To Be Good To Yourself* remarks

"Don't let anyone "should" on you. Don't we do that? Then, when other people get through "should-ing" on us, we "should" on ourselves. What happens next? If we don't do all of those "shoulds," we feel guilty! Do you know what guilt is? It is nothing more than excess emotional baggage. Guilt is a lot like worry, and worry is like sitting in a rocking chair: it gives you something to do but it doesn't take you anywhere."

Thank you, Donna!

Other Language No-No's

Other language no-no's are: "It's a killer," "I'd die to have that," or "I'd kill to have that," also, "I love him to death." Think of all the negative cues you are giving yourself by using such language. It would be just as acceptable to say "It's a very hard job," "I'd love to have that," or "I just adore everything about him."

The object is to bring your feelings in line with your communications and to get your heart and mind in sync with your desires. Whatever is driving your accumulation of clutter, I know you want to get a handle on it and infuse your life with ways to move forward and change. Clear and positive ways of speaking result from the inner work you are doing. Language is always the result of your thoughts, habits, and inner directives. It has power to influence you and others positively or negatively. As you incorporate many of the hints and ideas in this book into your life, you will undoubtedly also change your speech and thinking patterns.

Notice that nowhere in this book do I use terms such as: attack, conquer, beat, vanquish, kill, battle, fight, assault, make war, shoot down, blast away, or combat to describe ways to address your clutter. We need more peace and calm in our lives. Why add to the messes and chaos with violent, war-like speech? Describing your clutter clearing in this manner gets in the way of establishing a peaceful and harmonious internal and external environment. Thinking positive thoughts and using positive language is important to establishing the kind of life you desire for yourself.

What Can I Do to Change My Habits and Old Ways of Thinking and Doing Things?

Scan the following list and pick three items to work into your daily thoughts and activities. Later, return to this list and try three more items until you have done all of them. As you adopt these new thought patterns you will begin to notice a subtle or sometimes great difference in the way you think, make decisions and purchases, as well as a newfound ability to plan and execute a space-clearing project. (Also refer to the box "Taking a look at your shopping practices" on page 20.)

- Realize that clutter clearing is an ongoing process that takes place every day.

- Realize that clutter is an outward symptom of procrastination, weak boundaries, and problems with decision-making.

- Think more about the abundance in your life and not the lack.

- Be more purposeful and conscious of your choices and decisions.

- No one is saying you have to do a particular task; you make the choice to do it or not.

- Pay attention to the details of your life and begin to live consciously.

- Remember everything you bring into the house has to be taken care of.

- It is important to get rid of everything that does not give you a "yes" when you ask "Do I love it or can I use it?"

- How much of your stuff does not contribute to your comfort, efficient living, or joy?

Things To Think About

1. Use visualizations such as those found in Chapter 15.

2. Are you secretly afraid of getting organized?

3. Try to spend quality time alone and enjoy the gift of quiet.

CHAPTER 4

Reactions to Clutter

᭳ QUIZ

1. Do you save parts to unknown things?

2. Do you save broken things intending to fix them and never do?

3. Do you put things in places you know aren't right, telling yourself "it's just for now?"

4. Have you run out of storage space?

5. Are you so ashamed of your home that you have stopped entertaining?

In this chapter l address some of the deeper emotions that cluttering produces. Anger, anxiety, a feeling of helplessness, and angst over feelings that are tied to your stuff, create emotional issues that need to be addressed. Excuses are generated which distance you from dealing with the messes. Understanding these emotions and finding ways to change your actions and thoughts are important to consider when clearing the clutter from your life. Anger, anxiety, and helplessness get in the way of your ever being able to break free from the messes that have caused so much chaos and stress in your life. Let's confront them and then change them to more positive behaviors.

Learned Helplessness

Learned helplessness often takes root as a reaction to clutter. Some feel that nothing they do will make a difference, so they do nothing. Many engage in the avoidance behavior of distracting themselves from the important work they have to do with various forms of entertainment. Resistance to structured activities, and claiming an inability to focus on anything long enough to make any effective changes are some other ways learned helplessness shows up. In Chapter 5, I offer some solutions for these behaviors.

Clutterers Produce Excuses

Excuses commonly stated for not doing anything about your clutter.

1. I don't have the time
2. I don't have the skills.
3. I don't have the patience.
4. It's not all my stuff.
5. It won't make a difference—it will come back again.

6. I don't have enough space for everything.

7. I have always been messy.

8. I come by it rightly, my mother was a pack rat.

9. I will make the time next week or when I get a few days off.

More excuses commonly heard for not getting rid of something that has exceeded its usefulness:

1. I paid a lot for it.

2. I might need it in the future.

3. It was a gift from someone.

4. It's been in the family for a long time.

5. It might come back in style.

6. I'm just storing it for the kids.

7. I might fix it someday.

These are all good excuses and have served people well over the years. They don't, however, get you any closer to solving the seemingly insurmountable obstacles you see every day in your surroundings. Are you ready for the work involved in going over all your stuff and making the hard decisions? In the following chapters you will find many helpful and quick ways to get going with some changes you have no doubt wanted to make for a long time. Help is on the way.

CLUTTER SLOWS DOWN THE ENERGY IN THE ENVIRONMENT
AND IS A SYMBOL OF BEING HELD BACK.

Clutter Produces Anger

Students in my classes remark that they carry around a lot of anger towards themselves with regard to their messy surroundings. They seem to hang onto this negativity instead of moving towards positive choices and report that it is hard to turn the corner, accept themselves, and eliminate feelings of guilt and embarrassment and the tendency to live in the past. For this reason, I also offer suggestions for rewarding and taking care of yourself during and after completing projects. Look in Chapter 16 pages 131–133. Approach your space-clearing projects as a way to midwife yourself. Nurturing and caring for your needs is one of the missing links in a thorough look at clutter clearing. (I also refer you to the help on pages 123–125.) As you start completing projects that clear your mess and make your spaces more comfortable and inviting, you will experience your anger transforming into more positive emotions that help you approach life's challenges.

Clutter Produces Anxiety

Clutter all by itself produces a tremendous amount of anxiety. As many of my students and clients have said, "It's always an irritant, and it's always there, on my mind." Add to that the stress and tension of not having a space to live or work in that is conducive to clear thinking, creative endeavors, and general well-being and you have several good reasons why some people never start to clear their clutter.

Even when you are going about your daily activities, clutter and your inability to tackle the mess is always on your mind, making you feel guilty. These feelings are suppressed, pushed away, and not allowed to come to the surface. The more you repress feelings about clutter, the more you become uneasy and anxious.

Anxiety also produces fuzzy thinking and decreases your ability to focus clearly. This delays you from getting started on space clearing and carrying out projects that need a clear mind and a positive attitude.

Clutter produces anxiety and anxiety then produces more clutter. It is important to decide to break out of this cycle and embark on a plan to create the environment you desire and deserve.

On a very basic and elemental level, your body is uncomfortable with the chaos that clutter brings with it. The stress and anxiety that clutter produces affects you on a very basic cellular level. Cells exist in an orderly environment. When that ceases, disease takes over, and on a very primal level you resist that. Your body is automatically driven to create health, balance, and calm. Listen to your body: Is it sending you messages?

Relationships With Your Stuff

You have relationships with your things and the thought of chucking them out produces more anxiety. It is as though you are throwing away a part of yourself, and that is very difficult to do. Consciously deciding whether you want to continue having a relationship with every item that surrounds you will encourage you to live with more purpose, intention, and consciousness. Establishing new ways of behaving, speaking, and thinking in your daily life will enable you to make the hard choices that space clearing demands.

Clearing out stuff that has hung around for a long time in your home or work space can trigger emotions that will rise to the surface and have to be dealt with on many levels.

You may be hanging onto things that bring up fears about the future, regrets about the past, and feelings of inadequacy about the present. Getting rid of items that have no observable use and take up valuable space can open the door for new ideas, relationships, and opportunities to enter your life.

Many people store projects they have wanted to do, hobbies they hoped to get started on, even ideas for a new career. Clearing these out may feel like reneging on your closely held dreams and aspirations. They may also be telling you it's time to move on to more realistic goals.

Getting rid of former loved ones' possessions can bring up feelings of not having done the right thing or not having done enough for those relationships. It may feel as though love has evaporated from your life. Without these items you are not physically reminded of those past experiences. Happy memories can still live on in your heart and the others can be dealt with.

You may have grown up in a home that was mired down in depression-era thinking that there was never enough and therefore it was essential to stock up and store for the future. Unfortunately

> "DEFINITION OF PROACTIVE: ACTING FROM THE BELIEF THAT
> WE ARE RESPONSIBLE FOR OUR OWN LIVES AND HAVE THE FREEDOM
> TO CHOOSE OUR BEHAVIOR. YOU PREPARE AND SHAPE
> EVENTS RATHER THAN REACT TO THEM.
>
> —*The Complete Idiot's Guide to Organizing.*

that mindset in today's world makes it all too easy to shop, be enticed by offers, and buy unnecessary stuff. Be assured that it is possible to replace almost anything today. There are collectors, E-bay, and journals that expressly cater to old-timey things and objects you may have thought were no longer available.

People who are able to make hard decisions about their stuff trust that they will make good choices and have no regrets from letting go of things that no longer serve them. They know making room for something equal or better to take their place opens the door to new possibilities and opportunities. Maturity is the factor here. We come to realize that letting go is the best thing we can do for ourselves.

❧ TIP ❧

IT'S JUNK IF:

- It's broken, obsolete, or fixing it is unrealistic.
- You've never used it.
- It's the wrong size, color, or style.
- Using it is a bother.
- It would not easily affect you if you never saw it again.
- You have to clean it, store it, and insure it, but you don't get much enjoyment out of it.*

*Source: These are from Don Aslett, who has written
many wonderful books about clutter clearing.

This chapter takes you through the many reactions to clutter and several solutions for eliminating them in your life and environment. Remember, a positive frame of mind is important when embarking on clutter clearing and even when reading about it. You are attempting to break through many years of habits, behaviors, and choices that are presently not serving you. You have to start somewhere. It is imperative to understand cluttering behaviors and hallmarks before going any further with the changes you need.

Things To Think About

1. The clutter around you creates blockages, stagnant, swampy, sticky, icky areas in your home and your life.

2. Your clutter did not appear in a day and will not go away in one day.

3. The time you spend looking for things can never be reclaimed ... it is lost forever.

4. Become acutely aware of your surroundings.

CHAPTER 5:

Clearing Mental Clutter

℘ QUIZ

1. Is there so much chaos around you that you can't think clearly?

2. Are you involved with more activities and have more commitments than you really have time for?

3. Are you hesitant to try new ideas?

Spring Cleaning Your Life involves looking into all the ways you think, feel, and nurture yourself, not just looking at the physical clutter around you. You will begin to see that your mind, emotions, and spiritual life are directly connected to the physical clutter in your home or office. Physical clutter will begin to fade away as you tend to the way you think, process your emotions, and feed your soul. Your choices will change, as will your buying and storing habits. Time will feel less rushed and your housekeeping chores will become easier. Suddenly, you will discover that you are thinking more clearly and feeling less guilty. These new practices, habits, and attention to your thought and speech patterns will result in fewer piles, less stuff to take care of, and a home that nurtures all its members.

It's not easy to change old habits, clear old self-talk tapes, and embark on new ways of thinking. Be patient with yourself. I suggest choosing one area of frustration. Try several solutions, gain some clarity, and reap the benefits. Then try a few more, gradually working through your most pressing forms of clutter.

What Is Mind Or Mental Clutter?

Mental clutter takes hold when anxiety, fear, or chaos in your life intrudes into thinking, planning, and decision making. These states of mind interfere with your ability to perform complex mental tasks and also decrease your ability to bring your mind to a state of rest.

How does mental clutter begin to accumulate and influence the amount of physical clutter around you?

When your life is filled to overflowing with meetings, social activities, and obligations of all sorts, your mind gets very little rest. Your life takes on a chaotic nature and you quickly become overwhelmed with the amount of clutter that begins to accumulate.

Diversions of all sorts start to look attractive, and take you away from finding time and energy to tend to the mounting piles.

Making decisions and starting and completing projects get even harder. Too much TV, violent and noisy videos, video games, and CD's add to the chaos. This incessant chatter limits your thought processes and saps your creativity. Are you beginning to understand how all these forms of chitter-chatter lead to increased pressure in your life?

Your mind wanders and jumps around from thought to thought, creating even more distraction. You may give up even before you start because each project seems monumental under these conditions.

Negative speech patterns (as discussed on pages 22–24 in Chapter 4) also add clutter to your mind and make clear communication difficult. This foments even more disorder. As your boundaries weaken, it's even more difficult to say "no" and the use of negative speech patterns such as "I'd kill to have that" take over. Your mind becomes even more burdened by old self-talk tapes and feelings of guilt. Returning phone calls, writing letters, or keeping up with due dates of all kinds fall to the wayside.

Pressure and stress build up, leaving little time for dreaming, planning, or making changes that you sorely need and desire. Mental pathways are clearly in trouble, confusion is rife, and you have given up on ever making changes that will allow your life to run smoothly.This background brings on more physical clutter than you already have because you don't know where or how to start bringing order out of the mental or physical chaos.

Some Quick Ways To Alleviate Mental Clutter

- ❏ Start to keep and write in a journal.

- ❏ Do yoga or tai chi.

- ❏ Schedule 5–10 min breaks every 1½ or 2 hours.

- ❏ Look out a window occasionally.

- ❏ Take a short walk.

Try The Following

1. *Focus on the future*

Focus on where you want to be and what you want to do, not where you were and who did what, when. Create a clear mental image of your goals and dreams, then take whatever action you can to move in that direction.

2. *Make a list of those things you do best**

Consider your skills, abilities, strengths, special gifts, or things you have a knack for doing. You have some or possibly all of these and need a boost to your self-confidence. Become aware of them by making a list to refer to when you feel down or unable to go forward with your projects.

*Source: Read Now, Discover Your Strengths by Marcus Buckingham and Donald O. Clifton, PhD. This book will help you identify your five dominant talents and develop these into personal strengths.

YOU ARE A LIVING MAGNET OF THE LAW OF ATTRACTION.
WHAT YOU THINK YOU ATTRACT.

3. *Create a life collage*

Cut pictures from your favorite magazines that show how you want your life to be, that image some of your goals, and that depict relationships and actions that you want in your life. Paste them on a stiff board and place it where you can see it all the time. It will remind you of your goals and the changes you wish to make. It will keep you on target and draw to you the things that you desire. At the end of one year, evaluate what on your board has been fulfilled. Make a new board every year that reflects your new desires, visions, and goals. Seeing your dreams every day will help make them become real.

The subconscious mind cannot tell the difference between a real experience and one that you vividly imagine. So imagine your goals.

Following is from Brian Tracy, *Maximum Achievement.*

❑ When you create a collage, you are creating a powerful visual representation of your goals. This symbolizes success and achieving your plan to you and your subconscious mind.

❑ Take some time every day to stand in front of this collage and drink in the images and dwell on the positive ideas presented.

❑ An improvement in your life begins with an
improvement in your mental pictures.

❑ This enables you to cancel negative habits, thoughts, and
behaviors that have not served you well over the years.

❑ Eventually your subconscious mind will transfer the
positive feeling associations to your conscious mind.
Your fears will gradually diminish and eventually
disappear.

4. Use breakthrough thinking

Breakthrough thinking is from *The Break-out Principle* by Herbert Benson, M.D. and William Proctor.

The Break-out Principle describes a plan that helps to change prior mental patterns and open a door to personal benefits, including spiritual development, greater mental acuity, and increased productivity.

❑ One learns from struggling with a knotty problem "to
pull the trigger" and then experience a resolution.

❑ Some triggers are helping others, gardening, knitting,
walking in the woods, exercise, or taking a hot bath.

❑ The cycle ends with you reaching a state of improved
performance, personal breakthroughs, and/or new
mind-body patterns.

If you can learn which triggers work for you to resolve problems, you can improve your reactions to them and change long-held habits and ways of thinking that have kept you locked into old ways of behaving.

5. Use visualization techniques

Use visualizations to flood your mind at every opportunity with pictures of your ideal space, life, or job. See Chapter 15 for more ideas.

6. Examine your beliefs

Look for negative things you hear yourself saying such as:

"I can't", "I always", "If only".

Replace these with positive language:

"I can", "I will", "I could",etc.

Things To Think About

1. Act the part by doing very small projects successfully.

2. Feed your mind with reading, viewing, and listening to upbeat and proactive ideas.

3. Associate with positive people.

4. Teach others or tell others what you have learned and achieved. Teaching is the best way to learn; you become what you teach.

CHAPTER 6

Clearing Emotional Clutter

✒ QUIZ

1. **Do you resist change?**

2. **Are you so overwhelmed with your clutter that you don't know where to start?**

3. **Is your clutter a constant irritation in your life?**

4. **Do you stay busy in order to stuff your feelings and ignore them?**

What Is Emotional Clutter?

Emotional clutter prevents you from experiencing a full range of feelings. It makes ridding yourself of baggage from the past and resolving personal conflicts very difficult. Fear of the future and negative thoughts are some symptoms. The near relatives of fear are anxiety and stress, as well as mental upset. These states of

"I APPRECIATE WHAT HAPPENS INSTEAD OF COMPARING IT TO WHAT I THINK OUGHT TO HAPPEN."

Brian Tracy

mind cloud your ability to think clearly and create a mass of clutter in your mind and emotions.

People with emotional clutter tend to worry, criticize, and blame themselves and others. This habit can also lead to whining and complaining. Because they don't let go of old grievances, bitterness, and resentments, they are habitually living in the past, and they also have difficulty resolving anger, envy, family, or parental issues, and carry around a lot of old emotional baggage. Dealing inadequately with criticism or imagined slights adds to poor self-esteem and lack of self-confidence.

These issues are real for a lot of people and can fill emotional reservoirs with so much stuff (clutter) to take care of that it seems easier to throw up your hands and give up entirely as they can seem insurmountable.

How can you change this scenario? Try the following suggestions and begin to assess your level of stress as best you can for the moment. You may need to turn to professional help at some point. It can place things in perspective for you and pave the way to breaking through an impasse. Free-floating anxiety causes much distress and is treatable.

The emotional issues stated above are a form of clutter because they block you from finding happiness, well-being, and serenity. They limit your responses to situations, lead to poor problem solving, and create a background of ongoing stress that prevents you from attending to the physical clutter that accumulates when your emotions are pulled in many directions.

Some Quick Ways To Alleviate Emotional Clutter

❏ Ask yourself, "What am I feeling at this moment?"

❏ Get in touch with your feelings after an emotional upset. Figure out what caused your upset.

❏ Practice letting go of negative feelings or thoughts.

❏ Practice letting go of thoughts running around in your mind like a hamster on a wheel.

❏ Establish a new habit of thinking of several positive events of the day as you are driving home from work.

Other Emotional Issues That May Arise

1. Getting rid of clothes that don't fit and that you will never wear implies that you are accepting your present shape and state and will make better decisions in the future.

2. Getting rid of reading material that has piled up unread implies that you are giving up an interest you previously wanted to explore and makes room for exploring new interests.

3. Getting rid of stuff left over from former relationships implies that you have come to terms with loss and are moving on.

> "I FEEL HAPPY WHEN I WANT WHAT I GET.
> I FEEL SUCCESSFUL WHEN I GET WHAT I WANT."
>
> *Brian Tracy*

The following will bring a measure of emotional calm to your life and clear some mind clutter as well.

1. Lighten up and have fun.

2. Relieve intense emotions by addressing them rather than letting them build up.

3. Work on your driving habits to avoid adding more stress to your life.

4. Don't resort to drugs to sleep and to feel calm.

5. Spend time in nature.

6. Change habits that annoy others. You have control of yourself and what you do.

7. Work on strengthening boundaries that are weak.

8. Exercise.

---

1. **Try an Action Commitment** from Brian Tracy, *Maximum Achievement.*

Take a sheet of paper and make a list of all the things that you want to see in your life. Write down everything you can think of such as: good health, devoted family, interesting friends, financial success, respect from the community, chances to explore your dreams…use your imagination and let your mind wander freely and explore ideas.

For the next twenty-four hours, think and talk only about the things on your list. Do this when you go to sleep and when you wake up and then throughout the entire day. Create a day of only positive thoughts. No complaining, judging, worry, anger, or criticizing is allowed in this exercise. You will have to use your willpower to stay on target.

This exercise gives you insight into what it takes to maintain a positive and proactive attitude and to change a behavior. It will show you where you are in your progress on the road to changing and fixing your old ways of thinking, emoting, and valuing yourself and others.

2. *Seek out support groups* for any issue you wish to work on. This helps to boost self-esteem and offers ways to work with your problems. Plus, you will see that you are not alone.

3. *Therapy may also be a choice.* Don't overlook seeking medical help for free-floating anxiety, panic attacks, and severe stress. Medication may be needed to alleviate some behaviors or symptoms so that you can establish new habits and make progress in overcoming your symptoms. When your new habits are established, your need for medical treatment may diminish.

4. *Look into this book for help:* Ten Days to Self-Esteem by David D. Burns, M.D.

CLUTTER CAN SERVE AS A BUFFER,
SHIELDING US FROM OUR DEEPER ISSUES.

Things To Think About

The following steps will help to initiate change.

1. Be willing to change.

2. Say to yourself, "I want to change."

3. Be willing to make the effort.

CHAPTER 7

Clearing Spiritual Clutter

✒ QUIZ

1. **Do you understand the interconnection between the physical clutter in your life and the mental, emotional, and spiritual issues that are present?**

2. **Do you have a hard time breaking habits that no longer serve you?**

3. **When you look at your physical clutter do you understand how your mindset, emotional state of mind, and lack of self-nurturing have influenced your choices?**

What Is Spiritual Clutter?

Spiritual clutter limits your ability to fully develop values and actions that are in sync with, nurture, and support your purpose in life, your innermost desires, and your dreams. Spiritual clutter prevents consistent and conscious behavior and decision making.

Why does your spirit need any clearing? As your daily life unfolds, you lose track of your soul's needs. Why? Noise, clutter, stress, or chaos seep into your life and dim your ability to take care of your soul and your spiritual matters.

It is important to take responsibility for your cluttering ways. The truth is simple. You have spiritual clutter in your life because you have given attention to other matters rather than taking care of your surroundings, your thoughts, and your behaviors. Honesty with yourself about your goals is very important. Are you living your life in accord with your goals, desires, and values? When you aren't, tension and anxiety take over your life. This can keep you depressed and drained of the ability to think positively. Restoring consistency between your outer and inner worlds will help resolve all forms of clutter, restore your personal power, and elevate your self-esteem.

People are beginning to understand that their possessions have become a burden and a barrier to a satisfying spiritual life. Religious leaders and lifestyle coaches agree that an overabundance of material goods can become an impediment to spiritual development and happiness. People report they experience many inner rewards from clearing the clutter out of their life.

"THE GREATEST REVOLUTION OF MY LIFE IS THE DISCOVERY THAT INDIVIDUALS CAN CHANGE THE OUTER ASPECTS OF THEIR LIVES BY CHANGING THE INNER ATTITUDES OF THEIR MIND."

William James

Looking At How You Speak, Think, And Act

The ways you speak, think, and act impact your spiritual life. It is important to look deeply into how you speak, think, and act. Your body hears everything you say and can pick up negative images from your speech patterns. This can also influence your health.

Clear and positive ways of speaking are the results of your inner spiritual, emotional, and mental work. Language is always the result of your thoughts, habits, and inner directives and has the power to influence you and others positively or negatively.

You attract what you think about. Think more about the abundance in your life and not the lack.

The soul loves to actively participate in the goodness of life, its spiritual pursuits, and in feeding your core, your essence. If you rush about, live with too much stress, and give chaos a home in your life, you deny your soul a path to fulfilling your purpose in life.

When the motifs of your life consist of random choices or a lack of conscious living, then your thoughts, actions, and decisions can create barriers to the free flow of energy in your life, making it easy for physical clutter to accumulate.

Some Quick Ways To Alleviate Spiritual Clutter

❑ Meditate

❑ Pray

❑ Spend time in nature

❑ Find a like-minded spiritual community

Following are some deposits for your spiritual bank account. Visualize what you want your life to look like and more ideas will present themselves. Be sure to write these down and post them in places where you see them often. Visualize what life would be like if you instituted some of these ideas. Would you attract the friendships you desire? Would you feel less guilty because your values were expressed in your everyday decisions? Would you have more energy because bitterness and old grudges didn't weigh you down?

Here are some things to do that will get you thinking in the right direction. Go over these and refer back to them when you need to.

• Take a positive attitude towards life.

• Learn to forgive and forget.

• Let go of past experiences; don't let them continually go round and round in your mind.

"A GENUINE CONFRONTATION WITH THE TRUTH ... DEMANDS
AUTHENTICITY AND PERSONAL INTEGRITY. WHEN ONE FEELS ONE
WAY AND ACTS IN ANOTHER, ONE CREATES CONFLICT RATHER THAN
COHERENCE AND EXPERIENCES STRESS AND DISHARMONY OR DIS-EASE."

Frances Vaughn, The Inward Arc.

- Learn to let go of past grievances, bitterness, and resentments.
- Become aware of how your inner world is not in sync with your outer world.
- Learn to take risks.
- Decide to live in a manner consistent with your desires, goals, and values.
- Think more positively.
- Seek the valuable lesson in all situations.
- Simplify your life.

SOME QUESTIONS TO ASK YOURSELF:

- ❑ What areas of my life feel overextended?
- ❑ What creates the overwhelmed feeling?
- ❑ Do I feel trapped in a lifestyle that doesn't suit me?
- ❑ Watch to see where I am being pulled in two directions.
- ❑ Am I secretly afraid of slowing down? Will that mean I have to get to know myself better?
- ❑ Do I stay busy in order to stuff my feelings and ignore them?

The changes you make will be noticed by other people, so be prepared for comments that you are different, happier, or have more energy.

Brian Tracy offers the following suggestions for thinking more proactively and with a positive and hopeful attitude.*

1. *Think about the solution.* Focus on the solution rather than the problem. Solutions are inherently positive, problems are negative. The instant you think in terms of solutions, you become a positive and constructive human being.

2. *Look for the good.* Assume that something good is hidden within each difficulty or challenge. If you look for the gift, you will always find it. Dr. Norman Vincent Peale said, "Whenever God wants to give us a gift, he wraps it up in a problem."

3. *Seek the valuable lesson.* Assume that whatever situation you are facing at the moment is exactly the right situation you need to ultimately be successful. This situation has been sent to you to help you learn something, to help you become better, to help you expand and grow.

4. *Decide to be positive.* Use your mind to exert mental control over the situation. You will end up being positive and cheerful most of the time.

*Source: Brian Tracy from an article on **www.mercola.com**

I discovered in my research and in listening to my students that many of the same solutions work for mental, emotional, and spiritual clutter. That makes it a lot easier to do something about all of them. It appears that the three are very interrelated, stem from many of the same issues, and have some of the same causes. With that in mind, I have presented several solutions. Any of them will probably work. Try all, or pick and choose for specific problems.

If you are a pack rat or procrastinator, look into the chapter with help for these behaviors. Many mental, emotional, and spiritual forms of clutter come from and are related to these unresolved issues.

You no doubt have said to yourself a thousand times, "If only I could get a handle on these problems." Perhaps you didn't realize how related they all were, especially how interconnected mental, emotional, and spiritual clutter are to your physical clutter. You will see how all the forms of clutter impact each other. I feel sure when this occurs you will have made a giant leap towards clearing all the clutter and decreasing your irritation and stress. We rarely talk about mental, emotional, and spiritual forms of clutter. They are hidden and pushed aside in the mad rush of space clearing and re-organizing. Now you can see them for what they are and also understand how they influence the accumulation of piles, stuff, and junk.

Things To Think About

1. What do you want?

2. Do you know what feeds you?

3. Do you know what is most important to you?

PART 2

GETTING DOWN TO THE NITTY GRITTY

CHAPTER 8

Pack Rats and Procrastinators

✒ QUIZ

1. **Do you keep newspapers, magazines, or catalogs for months, even years?**

2. **Do you go shopping to ease your anxiety?**

3. **Do you keep things long past their usefulness?**

Pack Rat

The pack rat keeps (for years) all kinds of catalogs, magazines, newspapers, unopened mail, and just about anything. Things are stored that have no observable use. Unable to throw anything away, pack rats often live amidst piles of possessions that serve almost as a fortress of protection. Firemen in New York City found a man buried in his apartment. They were unable to get to him for two days and finally had to dig him out from under all his stuff. Are you snickering because you have sometimes thought this could happen to you? It is real for millions in this affluent nation of ours.

Your shelves let out a groan every time you go by, overstuffed folders are lying everywhere, and you are incapable of throwing anything away. Some professionals in the field say that these behaviors show fear of the future, stubbornness about letting go, and an inability to change long-standing behaviors and habits that no longer work.

Others say that pack rats have invested emotional meaning in their stuff, including unopened mail. They have a tendency to view their possessions as parts of themselves. More possessions denote there is more to the person, and help increase self-esteem. Loneliness, few friends, reduced contact with society in general, and not enough exercise or activity imparts an "I can't change" attitude to the pack rat's life, and this attitude hardens over time.

Many pack rats live alone and others are part of families that tolerate their behavior because there is still enough room for their stuff. My students have told me that many are in marriages where their spouse saves just about everything, using up all available space and creating a fire hazard. What's to be done?

Pack rats have difficulty seeing the abundance and opportunity that exists around them. Storing unread materials, living with piles of magazines, newspapers, and catalogs, gadgets, stacks of unopened mail, and boxes of stuff gives them a feeling of protection and a sense of good fortune.

Pack rats often go shopping to relieve anxiety. Anxiety temporarily goes away on a shopping trip, going through catalogs, ordering from the internet, or buying from TV ads. Literature in the field shows that pack rats experience a deep sense of inadequacy in their lives, leading to overbuying, overeating, and overreacting. Many studies reveal that pack rats suffer from poor self-esteem and boundary issues and use their shopping trips and purchases to boost their self-image. Of course, this doesn't work, and only fills their spaces with possessions they neither need nor can afford.

It would help pack rats to understand they are using their piles as walls or barriers to intimacy and relationships with the world. Possessions replace relationships and effective communication skills. The stuffed, stagnated, and blocked feeling of the unending piles and boxes also prevents good decisions, clear thinking, and the release of old habits and thought patterns.

Some pack rat behaviors stem from old messages and thought patterns such as:

- It's a sin to throw anything away.
- I may use it someday.
- Aunt Velma gave it to me.
- It has been in my family for generations.
- Maybe the kids will want it?
- Waste not, want not.
- Did I get my money's worth?

Many people have not yet adjusted to the demands of the 21st century and our tendency to become inundated with paper, possessions, and piles. These savers fear that every little thing is useful and will be needed someday for something. A woman in one of my classes came to me almost in tears about her husband's need to keep forty years of *National Geographic* magazines neatly stacked in the basement. They were never looked at, read, or used in any way. I suggested they be given to a school, library, hospice, or charity. Keeping one dozen of the best issues and the indexes (you can find any issue in a library) can be a good solution to this common problem.

I have met people who have large stashes of sweaters, shoes, purses, hats, books, and/or collectibles of all kinds. They exhibit no concern about the masses of possessions that could not possibly be used in fifteen lifetimes and the impossible need to find available space to store them properly. They report loving their collections and don't want to change. There is little a consultant can do about this type of behavior, since there appears to be no discomfort associated with it. They enjoy their collections and wish to live with them.

SOLUTIONS FOR THE PACK RAT

- Work with your anxiety and stress by learning meditation and visualization techniques.

- Seek help to confront your fears.

- If your anxiety and stress symptoms are severe, consider seeing a doctor and the possibility of medication. This may give you the relief that will allow you to work on your clutter.

- Seek help to boost your self-esteem, such as counseling, reading, support groups, and friends to share your progress and accomplishments.

- Read everything you can find about your condition, while being absolutely honest with yourself. Knowledge leads to freedom and choice.

- Seek more spiritual outlets, such as Unitarian Universalist or Unity congregations, meditating, support groups, and prayer for help.

- Embark on space-clearing projects, scheduled in small 15-30 minute segments, that will lead to recycling, donating, and selling much of the stuff that is crowding your living space.

- Focus on one project at a time. Set aside small segments of time, such as 15 minutes, for your projects.

- Go through your subscriptions to magazines, journals, newspapers, and catalogs and eliminate those not needed or never read. Pull out specific articles to read and put them in a folder labeled "TO READ."

- Take charge of your time and manage it with care.

- Instead of saying "I have always been this way" say "I am making changes and it will take some time."

- Visualize your home as you would like it to be. Return to this image every evening just before you fall asleep.

- Resolve not to go shopping to alleviate anxiety, to be with friends, for entertainment, or to relieve boredom.

- Learn to let go of stuff that no longer serves you.

- Reward yourself after completing a project or for habits changed and maintained with a luxurious bubble bath, a dinner with a friend, or a rented movie. Pick inexpensive or free things for your reward.

Please remember that pack rats may suffer from ADHD (attention deficit/hyperactivity disorder), ADD (attention deficit disorder), OCD (obsessive compulsive disorder), or from chronic anxiety. Many may need medication for these conditions. It is important to consult with an appropriate health professional for any of these disorders if you suspect that you have the symptoms. The symptom list can be seen on many of the sites listed in the *Resources* at the end of this book. Here are some of them:

- ❑ Trouble wrapping up the final details of a project once the challenging parts have been done.

- ❑ Difficulty keeping things in order.

- ❑ Difficulty remembering appointments or obligations.

- ❑ Avoids getting started with projects that require organization and thought.

- ❑ Fidgety or squirming hands or feet.

- ❑ Mind wanders easily.

❧ QUIZ

1. Do you feel you do your best work under pressure?

2. Do you feel you must do everything perfectly?

3. Do you come from a family of overachievers?

Procrastinators

What makes people accumulate clutter? Could it be the way our brains are wired? Why are some born to neatness and order and others just can't seem to keep things organized? The library and bookstores are filled to overflowing with wonderful titles that help, yet the clutter never seems to end. I believe that some of it stems from our culture and the way we live and think.

In this chapter I have chosen to discuss the nature of some of the most intractable cluttering problems. Truth to tell, we all exhibit some of these characteristics.

At the outset, let me say that there is hope for all of these behaviors. They can be eradicated completely if you work on them. It does take a good deal of time, effort, and thought. Let us embark on this journey together. I hope my ideas will help you.

A procrastinator may not necessarily possess all of the following characteristics. They may have two or three and still find themselves beset with this troublesome issue. I do not intend to imply that all procrastinators exhibit all of the descriptions. In fact, if the truth were told, most of us have done one or more of these at one time or another.

Putting off chores for the last minute and perfectionism are the main symptoms of this very painful problem. Procrastination is a choice. You can overcome this pesky problem with new habits and choices.

Procrastinators often see deadlines as a fearsome aspect of their jobs. They create pressure by putting off assignments for the last minute. When the job finally gets done, they get a high that can become addictive. Objectivity and awareness of the deeper causes are obscured, overlooked, and avoided as they get the job done in the nick of time. Others create mental diversions to ease the discomfort they feel. They shift between the excuses of fear of failure and fear of success for not doing things in a timely manner. Many procrastinators are always late and deny that this is avoidance behavior, remarking, "Oh, that's the way I am," without considering others' needs.

Some procrastinators come from families where overachievement and conformity were modeled and perfection was demanded. Their parents emphasized competition and compared their grades and behavior at school with their friends. Life became stressful and remained so into adulthood. They responded with rebellion against authority and structure. It can help to find other ways to rebel, such as dressing funky on the weekends with friends, joining a drama group and becoming involved with being the person you are playing, or volunteering with a social change organization. Adopt a healthy pursuit of excellence, eliminate the fear of making mistakes, and view failure as an opportunity to grow and learn.

Procrastinators may find closeness hard to tolerate and starting and keeping relationships may be uncomfortable because of feelings of imperfection and fears of being exposed. At the same time, procrastinators often demand perfection. When a procrastinator must face a new task, their core is threatened and they become fearful and anxious.

Finally, procrastinators postpone jobs for the perfect moment, which, of course, never comes. Piles of papers and clutter sit waiting for the perfect time to be put away. They often put off a task that would ordinarily take one-quarter of the time. If they can't do a job perfectly, they won't do it at all. Procrastinators frequently expect more of themselves than is realistic, find any excuse to postpone a task or go to an easier or less onerous one, and convince themselves the task will be easier in the future.

Procrastinating behaviors are perpetuated and strengthened by our culture, which broadcasts messages that we all must be perfect, imposes excessively high standards, and teaches us to pursue success at any cost. Learning that it is okay to fail, blunder, and make mistakes is good.

❧ TIP ❧

Remember that spending fifteen minutes a day on almost any project will mean completion very soon. Breaking the task into small doable segments makes it easy to accomplish. Writers do this. They write for one hour a day, and within a month can have a short story or assignment completed without getting harried and frustrated. Rome was not built in a day.

Five Reasons You Might be a Procrastinator

1. You find it hard to make lists and prioritize.

2. You are overwhelmed with work and let things pile up.

3. You do work you don't enjoy or are bored.

4. You feel uncertain and doubt yourself.

5. You are easily distracted.

REMEMBER THAT PROCRASTINATION IS A CHOICE.
YOU CAN LEARN TO FORGIVE YOUR FAMILY AND YOURSELF AND
CHANGE YOUR HABITS, THOUGHT PATTERNS, AND BEHAVIOR.

THE DOWN AND DIRTY RULES
TO GET RID OF PROCRASTINATION FOREVER

- Commit to doing one project.

- Make an appointment with yourself and write it on your calendar.

- Break your project down into small, manageable, obtainable segments.

- Write down the entire project on a piece of paper, creating steps to follow from beginning to end.

- Commit to at least 15 minutes on the project. Do one task, such as organizing one drawer, half of a file, one cabinet, or the first three steps in a chosen project.

- Assemble all your supplies to complete the job

- Every day, do something towards completing the project.

- Do the hardest thing first or try the easiest thing first. Discover which way works best for you

- Visualize every step needed to complete the project. Visualize the completed project in the morning and the evening before retiring.

- Do the first step and work for 10 minutes. Now, you realize it's not as difficult as you thought it would be, nor did it take as long as you thought it would.

- Enlist a buddy to call when you are working on a project to help keep you motivated.

- Commit publicly to doing the project.

- Remember to reward yourself each time you complete a project on time.

Seek help from these two books: *Ten Days To Self-Eteem* by David D. Burns, M.D. Chapters 8 & 9 and *The Now Habit* by Neil Fiore, PhD.

Things To Think About

1. Learn to feel your discomfort and decide where in your body you feel this. Concentrate on this feeling for 10 minutes. Simply acknowledge the feelings, and then go on to the job at hand. Your physical symptoms will probably disappear.

2. Write down three reasons you put off doing things. Post your reasons where you can see them.

3. Set achievable goals. No pie in the sky dreams.

4. Be patient with yourself. It takes effort and time to break lifelong habits.

5. Look at tasks as challenges rather than as threats.

CHAPTER 9

Grasshoppers and Untidy Folk

☙ QUIZ

1. Do you interrupt your clutter cleaning work to make a phone call or begin a different task?

2. Do you stop a task before you are done because you are bored or need a change?

3. Do you become easily distracted and unfocused if the task becomes too difficult?

Grasshoppers

Grasshoppers flit from project to project. After starting work on one task they are frequently attracted to other piles or tasks. Cleaning, organizing, and rearranging other areas beckon while they are engaged in a chosen job.

Before completing the task of the moment, they think of a thousand other things to do. These other tasks somehow look more attractive. Grasshoppers leave the pile half sorted, the shelf half organized, or the closet partly rearranged.

Jumping from one project to another creates frustration, confusion, and upset. This behavior also leaves countless tasks half done and more difficult to finish. Grasshoppers usually tackle the easier tasks first, leaving the more difficult ones for last. They also have difficulty prioritizing and a hard time focusing on one job at a time. They believe the job at hand is more difficult and time-consuming than the task distracting them. Or, the thought of tackling a difficult project is too overwhelming. Whatever the reason, sticking to one project until it is completed presents a challenge.

SOLUTIONS

- It is essential that you make a list of your projects. Then prioritize them on another list and post it.

- Schedule time on your calendar to do the first item on your list. Writing it down will help cement your commitment.

- When you start the project, turn off the TV and resolve to not answer the phone (let your answering machine pick it up and call back later).

- Use a kitchen timer to keep track of the time you have allotted for the project. Don't stop until the timer goes off.

- Play upbeat music.

- Learn to relieve the tension you feel when embarking on a new project by visualizing your project completed and meditating to reduce stress.

- Take a walk before you start on your project, do some yoga, garden for a bit, burn an aromatherapy candle, open windows and doors to let in fresh air and natural light, or call a friend to help you over the rough spots.

✑ QUIZ

1. Do you label yourself a messy or disorganized person?

2. Do you have piles of clothes on the floor of your closet and bedroom?

3. Do you have trouble retrieving important papers or keys?

Untidy Folk

Sometimes people are labeled untidy or messy when they are young and keep the label into adulthood. Perhaps you think there is no hope for you. Perhaps you believe you are untidy due to ADHD, or you may have come from a family that was ultra-neat and you are now rebelling. Your lifestyle may be so stressful and fast-paced that you have little time (or so you think) to keep things neat and picked up. Your home may be so cluttered that you don't have adequate space to keep things orderly. This stress, coupled with the clogged space, creates a lack of ability to focus on the task at hand. As the piles increase, the job becomes insurmountable, and you end up doing nothing about your mess.

You are desperate to change your situation. You know that being so messy is the main cause of stress in your life. You can't find anything, are embarrassed to have friends over, and can't find space to put things away. Here are some solutions.

SOLUTIONS

- Visualize your home or office as you would like it. Return to this image before you retire each evening and again in the morning.

- Time management is a good thing to read about (Chap.11).Try to use some of the principles in your life.

- Make a commitment to change your habits of throwing things on the floor and not putting things away.

- You can choose to be neat by establishing new habits.

- Write down the habits you wish to change.

- Write down the specific habits that make you disorganized.

REMEMBER THAT THIS IS ALL ABOUT CHOICE AND NOT ABOUT CHORES.

- Banish the word "failure" from your vocabulary.

- Don't compare your home or your progress to others.

- Instead of saying, "I have always been this way" say "I am making changes and it will take some time."

- Release yourself from your past; anyone can change when they want to.

- Essentially, becoming tidier is a commitment to changing long held patterns and self-talk tapes that play over and over again in your head.

- Become more aware of untidy areas in your surroundings. Write down each one and what you can do to create and keep neatness in that area.

(Please also refer to page 65 and the paragraph on ADHD.)

❧ TIP ❧
SMAC

S = SIMPLE, KEEP IT SIMPLE

M = MANAGEABLE, KEEP IT MANAGEABLE

A = ACCOMPLISH, KEEP IT SOMETHING YOU CAN ACCOMPLISH

C = COMPATIBLE, KEEP IT COMPATIBLE WITH YOUR TIME, ENERGY, AND SPACE

Things To Think About

Try to incorporate these into your new way of thinking. All are good for pack rats, procrastinators, grasshoppers, and untidy folk.

1. Resolve to do the job, even if it isn't perfect.

2. Start the habit of doing things right away.

3. STOP putting off for the right moment. The right moment is NOW.

4. Be open-minded and think out of the box to get the job done.

5. As you complete more and more projects on time, you will discover encouragement to do this again and again.

6. Remember that it takes 21 days to change an old habit.

7. Many consultants suggest the purchase of a kitchen timer to help you stick to your time allotments. The next job is to use it with each project.

CHAPTER 10

The Paper Chase

❧ QUIZ

1. **Are you drowning in paper?**

2. **Do you sort your mail immediately upon receiving it?**

3. **Do you have piles of papers on your desk, on counters, or on the dining room table?**

Most of my students tell me they are drowning in paper and can't see any end to it. The piles of paper produce a chaotic and depressing environment Chaos brings a lack of focus and loss of energy, and ends up taking your attention away from more important matters. Here are some hints to help you change the situation. Remember, today's mail is tomorrow's pile.

TO KEEP YOUR NEW-FOUND ORDER TAKE FIVE MINUTES AT THE END OF EACH DAY TO CLEAN UP YOUR SPACE AND GET ORGANIZED FOR THE NEXT DAY'S WORK. THIS CAN BE DONE AT WORK AND AT HOME.

Desk Disorder

To see an end to the piles of papers it is important to adopt new habits and behaviors.

- ❑ Don't make things too complicated.
- ❑ Store information ordinarily kept in your files on your computer.
- ❑ Those files and projects you are working with and that are now mixed with all the other papers on your desk require a special solution. Gather your working files and put them in a plastic box with a handle. Store it where you can use it when you want to work on your special projects. Or use a file holder that keeps your working files upright on your desk.
- ❑ Start to make a dent in the pile of papers that are left on your desk. Now at least you can see the top of the pile.
- ❑ Set aside just 15–30 minutes a day to, slowly but surely, go through these errant pieces of paper. File some, throw some away if you can, and deal appropriately with the rest.
- ❑ There. Now you can breathe easier and you can see the top and center of your desk.

The lesson in all this is to never mix projects with mail, papers, and other odds and ends. They become a jumble of confusion and chaos that will boggle your mind and not allow you to work with ease on either your filing or your projects. You deserve better. Take a deep breath and separate things slowly.

The Nine Basic Rules Of Paper

1. Make friends with your wastebasket.

a. As soon as you get it, throw away any mail you did not solicit or that is of no interest to you. Don't even open the envelope. Be severe with the mail. Recycle or throw away what you don't want, aren't interested in, or don't want to care-take. Handle mail as it comes in. Remember, the mail keeps coming six days a week and you will benefit from a system that disposes of most of it. Shredding is also a possibility.

b. When thinking about your papers consider the following designations: FILE, ACT ON LATER, or TOSS. Remember, file it, so you can find it.

c. Take the mail you decided to keep to your desk to sort into BILLS, FILING, ANSWER, or ACT ON LATER. Prepare folders, baskets, large bulldog clips, clipboards, separate drawers, or files to hold these categories.

2. Create a place to store your ACT ON LATER files and papers that is safe, secure, and accessible. You can go over these at odd moments.

3. Remember that papers begin to float if you haven't secured them firmly; that is, put them in their proper place. This of course, depends on you creating a system with a place for each kind of paper that comes into your space.

AT THE END OF EACH DAY MAKE A LIST OF SIX OF THE MOST IMPORTANT THINGS YOU HAVE TO DO AND NUMBER THEM IN ORDER OF IMPORTANCE. EACH MORNING BEGIN WITH THE FIRST ITEM ON YOUR LIST AND SCRATCH IT OFF WHEN YOU ARE FINISHED. WORK YOUR WAY DOWN THE LIST. IF YOU DON'T FINISH AN ITEM, PUT IT ON THE LIST FOR THE FOLLOWING DAY.

Donna Watson, PhD.

4. Ask yourself: "Do I wish to care-take and devote precious space to this piece of paper?" Can I access this information elsewhere, or is it available online? Try to keep the center of your desk clear.

5. Handle each piece of paper only once. Easier said than done, but try.

6. Establish a *paper management center* near where you open and read the mail. This could be your desk, since that is where your files and supplies are stored.

7. Realize that your world won't completely go to pieces if you throw out papers you absolutely don't want.

8. Decide what to do about all the catalogs, magazines, newspapers, and journals that you have saved. Cut out articles to read at a later time. Store in a TO READ file.

9. Resolve to only buy those magazines you are really interested in. Ask yourself why you subscribe to or buy this newspaper or magazine or keep that catalog. Are you in love with the photography, love the ideas, find the columns informative and interesting, or support the philosophy? Do you read it from cover to cover as soon as it arrives, or do you let the issue sit around until you get to it, or perhaps you never get to it?

❦ TIP ❦

1. Keep your papers moving along.

2. File, don't pile.

3. Give every item a home.

4. Purge often.

5. Reward yourself frequently.

Files

These are an important part of your paper management system. Value them. Alphabetize your hanging files, and within each file, put the most recent items in front. Indicate the drawer contents with a label on the outside. Also insert a card in your rolodex with this information on it, entitled FILE INDEX.

Remove paper clips from papers and use a stapler instead. Clips tend to fall off. Buy lots of manila folders for subcategories in your hanging files. Keep these labeled and up to date, adding more as it becomes necessary. Go over your files at least twice a year, weeding out those that you don't need any longer, readjusting your categories, and also cleaning out the contents of folders.

Important Documents

Here are some categories for important documents:

- ❏ Tax documents
- ❏ Insurance papers
- ❏ Active bank accounts
- ❏ Records of outstanding debts
- ❏ Retirement accounts
- ❏ Investment records
- ❏ Homeowners legal papers

Make a list of the documents in your safe deposit box. Keep important documents at home in a fire-proof box, a plastic file with a handle, or some container that works for you. Keep it easily accessible in case of an emergency.

Keep warranties and instruction manuals in your files. Attach the receipt to the warranty for proof of purchase.

Please refer to *Checklists for Life,* by Kirsten M. Lagatree. This book has a chapter on keeping documents.

Documents to Keep Forever

birth and death certificates

adoption papers

health records

marriage papers

divorce papers

military discharge papers

receipts for items bought

"Establish uninterrupted "quiet time" each day to accomplish specific tasks. You will have to make this happen because it will not happen accidentally.

Donna Watson, PhD.

Documents to Keep for a Limited Time
Tax records (seven years)
Check registers and bank statements (seven years)
Records to support tax returns (seven years)
Mortgage payments (seven years after property is sold)
Pay stubs (until W2 is confirmed at year end)
Property deeds (as long as you own the property)
Loan papers (seven years after the loan is paid off)
Auto titles and registration (as long as you own the car)
Appliance manuals (as long as the appliance lasts)

Keep to be Used for Tax Purposes
Copies of utility bills, credit card statements, expired insurance policies, and items relating to business expenses.

Ways To Reduce Your Junk Mail

You can join the Junk Mail Association for $20.00. They will delete your name from several direct marketing lists and lobby to protect your postal privacy. For $2.00 they will send you an information packet and an application.

■ Stop Junk Mail Association
c/o 3020 Bridgeway – Suite #150
Sausalito, CA 94965

■ National Waste Prevention Coalition in Seattle. Go to www.metrokec.gov/nwpc and click on "Reduce business junk mail."

■ You can also write to the Mail Preference Service, P.O. Box 9008 Farmingdale, NY, 22735-9008. This will eliminate a certain amount of junk mail.

■ Send for a booklet called *Stop Junk Mail Forever,* by Marc Eisensen from Good Advice Press, Elizaville, NY 12523 Telephone 914-458-1400.

Things To Think About

1. If I decide to keep this, how long will I have to keep it?

2. Where can I keep it so that I can find it easily?

3. Would I miss this if it disappeared?

4. Is there another place I can get this information?

CHAPTER 11

The Costs of Clutter

❧ QUIZ

1. Do you buy gadgets that take up valuable space in your closets or kitchen yet never get used?

2. Do you subscribe to magazines that are never read?

3. Are you storing items for friends, adult children, and/or organizations?

4. Have you been charged overdue payments for bills that got lost or misplaced?

5. Do you avoid cleaning because of the piles and boxes that are in your path?

When your life and environment are filled with clutter, time and money are wasted. I know you value these and wish to have more time and spend less money. What can you do? In this chapter, I outline ways to take control of your time and describe why storing and caring for clutter adds additional costs to your budget.

Time Management Ideas:

Feeling stressed from too many to-do's on your list? If you are being pulled in different directions and doing things for many people, you certainly need to change something to give yourself some relief.

FIVE RULES THAT WILL
HELP YOU MANAGE YOUR TIME*

1. Write down your goals.
   Here are some examples: (1) nurture myself more, (2) spend more quality time with my family, (3) work on my career.

2. Then eliminate responsibilities that don't directly contribute to your top three goals.

3. Re-evaluate your responsibilities at least twice a year and make the necessary adjustments.

4. Create a *time management chart* with three columns: (1) responsibilities, (2) approximate number of hours these take, and (3) which of your goals this responsibility helps you accomplish.

5. Learning to delegate is important. Your four-year-old can fold towels and easy things, while the eight- or nine-year-old handles the rest of the laundry.

---

*Source: *Indianapolis Woman*, August 2004, *Making Do With 24*, by Susan McKee.

After reviewing her chart, one of my clients decided to step down from two boards and stop acting as chair of the annual rummage sale for the PTA. She was able to take back 10–15 hours of her life each month, felt less stressed and rushed, and became more productive and happier with herself.

TRY SOME OF THE FOLLOWING TO EASE YOUR TIME CRUNCHES

- Don't bite off more than you can chew.

- Break complex tasks into manageable sections.

- Don't put off to tomorrow what you can do today.

- You can't organize your time until you know how you're spending it. Take a week and keep track of what you do every day.

- Visualize your goals. Where do you want to be 10 or 20 years from now?

- Establish a master calendar. Note every appointment and scheduled event.

- Plan for personal time on your calendar.

- Practice saying no and accepting only those jobs that lift your spirit.

- Reward yourself frequently for jobs completed.

Actually you can't afford not to organize. The extra cleaning that clutter creates takes time. Looking for things that get misplaced or lost, moving piles out of the way to clean around them or to get to other things behind or under the piles is a direct result of clutter in your surroundings. This costs you more valuable time.

The Real Cost Of Clutter

You are paying each month for storing, insuring, heating, cooling, cleaning, and care-taking your clutter.

Add up the extra space that a pile of newspapers and magazines take up. Could it be two square feet or is it three? Have you been storing these items for two months or even two years? Calculate the cost of this as part of your monthly expenses. Added up monthly for the year, this is a significant addition to your living expenses. What about the clothes you never wear, papers you have kept for twenty years, shoes that hurt your feet, and boxes in the garage that you have forgotten about?

Is this never used, overlooked, and dust-collecting excess using up 10% or even 20% of your available living space? Simple arithmetic shows that if you are paying $650 per month for rent or mortgage, you are paying $65 per month for storing your clutter, or $780 per year.

Jeff Campbell offers another formula to work with. Take each room separately and measure zones of clutter length by width to get the square footage. Then multiply by $1.00 per square foot. Another method is to price the cost of a rental unit to store your stuff and add that to your monthly expenses.

Areas of your home or office never get cleaned because it is just too difficult, so you skirt around them. Sometimes your home becomes unsafe because of boxes and piles you have to go around. They create narrow passages and sharp edges. Clutter tends to attract mites, dust, and bacteria that cause allergies, headaches, rashes, and a decrease in energy levels.

With organization, management, and critical thinking you can reduce your time losses and the cost of storing your clutter. Think about the ideas in this chapter, assess your own situation, and then implement some of the suggestions. You will feel much better as you gain control over valuable time and space in your life. When you estimate the various expenses that excess stuff creates, you will no doubt come to the conclusion that life is easier without so many possessions.

❧ TIP ❧

A Tub Tip

Put your projects—ongoing ones and those you want to get to—toys, tools, holiday decorations, hobbies and more in clear plastic inexpensive tubs. Label them clearly with colorful labels (buy a labeler). Stack them neatly out of the way. These things are ready to move when you are.

Things To Think About

1. Allow your space to support you. If your kitchen is organized you spend less time preparing meals.

2. Ask yourself what areas of your life feel overextended.

3. Ask yourself what creates the overwhelmed feeling.

4. Build a simple wardrobe. Black goes with everything. It will require less time to care for and less time choosing what to buy.

5. Pay your bills with automatic payments taken out of your bank account on a monthly basis. This reduces worry and time spent paying bills, and also the cost of stamps and envelopes.

PART 3

HOW TO
KEEP YOUR LIFE FREE OF CLUTTER, CALM, AND DELICIOUSLY EASY TO MAINTAIN

CHAPTER 12

Simplify Your Life

❧ QUIZ

1. **What parts of your lifestyle are distractions that keep you off pace and running ragged?**

2. **What can you cut out and still have an abundant life?**

3. **What are the stimulants that keep you wired?**

Groups are forming all over the country that center around moving towards simple living. Some are called "The Circle of Simplicity" and others "Voluntary Simplicity" groups. Why are people from all walks of life thinking about changes in their lives that support the values of simplicity? Many of my students report that material goods gobble up all their available time and money creating more things to clean, care-take, and store.

Simplifying your lifestyle can help clear the clutter. You will have less stress in your life and workplace with less clutter surrounding you, and more time to do the things you have wanted to do. There is nothing mysterious here. Owning less means less to store, clean, and be responsible for. Having more time creates less clutter because you aren't rushed and have more time to keep things organized. Minimalist thinking will begin to influence all your decisions, leading you to desire less and buy less.

Many people don't feel as secure in their jobs as they once did and are looking for ways to cut expenses and bring about long lost dreams of close family life, quality time spent with family members, and a life consistent with their values. They are seeking more control over their lives and the direction they are going

The American way is to own a huge house, far in excess of your needs, because you can, it's there to be had, and everyone else does. It takes two incomes to keep up with all the bills. The media do not just sell cars and homes, they sell self-esteem. Conjured up for the buyer is the premise that you will like yourself better if you own the hallmarks of our culture and also look the part. As a culture, we are clearly suffering from *affluenza.**

Affluenza and Escape from Affluenza—Television specials that explore the social and environmental costs of materialism and overconsumption: www.PBS.org/kcts/affluenza.

Doctors believe 80% of disease is caused by stress. Much of our stress is centered around the pace and needs of a job and lifestyle that are disconnected from peace and contentment. Barbara De Grotte-Sorenson and David Allen Sorenson report that, "Addicted to our own adrenaline, we sprinted from one meeting to the next."

The Sorensens examined their choices and decided to reduce everything involved with possessions. They wanted to play more with their children, reflect more, read more books, have more meaningful conversations, and value those things and activities they previously labeled a waste of time. Their life was out of sync with their true desires and filled with the clutter of too many possessions, too many credit cards, too many things to do and not enough time to do them, and too many choices about which meetings to attend. Moving towards wholeness while reining in their overextended lifestyle became their dream. In the course of changing and simplifying their lives they eliminated things that did not give them satisfaction or those that did not add to the quality of their life.

Students in my classes talk about how nice it would be to have their lives back. What does that mean? Rushing about day after day just to keep up is exhausting. Their homes are filled with possessions they don't use and the values they once cherished have been put aside. The dull ache of dissatisfaction and disillusion hovers over their daily lives. They have fallen for the American dream of buy now, pay later, take a loan out to pay your bills, get a new car every 2 or 3 years, and live well beyond your means.

Choosing intentional simplicity and creating a lifestyle that mirrored their true values and priorities was of prime importance. Home as a sanctuary for their family which reflected their mental, physical, emotional, and spiritual desires was part of that dream.

"OUTWARDLY SIMPLE, INWARDLY RICH."

Duane Elgin

QUESTIONS THE SORENSENS ASKED THEMSELVES:

- What are the values that guide my actions?

- What is my fair share?

- What is enough?

- Why don't I feel good?

- How can I integrate my feelings with my life choices?

- Who are my neighbors? Can we care more about our community and our neighbors? Will that give more quality to our lives?

- Why do we never seem to have enough time?

How Does Simplifying Reduce Clutter?

Simplifying your life and your choices brings many rewards. Most of all it brings back to your life ideals and dreams you once had.

1. Simplifying reduces how much you own, are responsible for, and maintain.

2. Simplifying gives you more room in your closets.

3. Simplifying increases free space in your home.

4. Simplifying clears mind chatter (mind clutter), giving you emotional, mental, and spiritual stability.

5. Simplifying keeps your home neater and more organized.

6. Simplifying keeps time under your control.

7. Simplifying creates peace and calm in your life, which gives you more energy.

Ideas For Changing Your Lifestyle:

- Eat out less.

- Wear your winter coat another season.

- Buy used.

- Reduce your entertainment bill. Do more with your children at home … play games, read together.

- Don't buy clothes that need dry cleaning.

- Simplify lawn maintenance or eliminate it entirely.

- Get rid of the cell phone.

- Work near where you live to eliminate or reduce commuting.

- Move to a smaller home to eliminate overextended finances.

- Consolidate bank accounts, get out of debt, go down to one credit card.

"SIMPLER LIVING INTEGRATES BOTH INNER
AND OUTER ASPECTS OF LIFE INTO AN ORGANIZED
AND PURPOSEFUL WHOLE."

Duane Elgin

- Slow down. Change your driving style Take your time while driving. Be patient on the road.

- Reduce Xmas expenditures. Try giving homemade items as gifts.

- Resign from organizations whose meetings you dread.

- Cook ahead and freeze. Grow your own food and preserve it.

- Reduce the amount of TV you and your children watch.

- Consider *time* a gift and value it.

- Create a household cleaning schedule, doing a little each day.

Things To Think About

1. Write down what you most long for.

2. Do a lifestyle survey.

3. Evaluate your time commitments.

4. Deal with unresolved conflicts, angers, and hurts before you start.

5. Where has your life clamored for de-cluttering?

CHAPTER 13

Setting Boundaries Helps Clear Clutter

❧ QUIZ

1. **Do people take advantage of you?**

2. **Do you communicate your feelings, needs, and desires?**

3. **Can you say "no" and be assertive to get your needs met and your time restraints understood?**

Setting boundaries has to do with knowing yourself better. When you are aware of and protect your boundaries you will be more in touch with your desires, needs, feelings, inner self, and intuition. This will help to reduce emotional clutter.

You can make a big change in your anxiety level and physical, mental, emotional, and spiritual clutter when you decide to work with your boundaries. By establishing and maintaining boundaries you accept responsibility for your own well-being.

It can be scary to set limits. Reminding yourself of the benefits you will experience can ease your concerns.The way others treat you will most likely change. You will now be able to state firmly what you expect and how you desire things to be done. This will reduce the clutter caused by others in your life. You will be more able to explain your limits about putting things back and loaning things, and more able to state your tolerance level for clutter created by others.

Some people have never thought of boundaries, let alone the need for establishing healthy ones. Unless you are clear and direct about what you need others will never know.

Without boundaries, you often allow others to treat you in ways that are convenient for them, not as you desire to be treated. Boundaries are necessary to let others know how you expect to be treated. You have only yourself to blame if you are taken advantage of by others. Being selfish in this way is a form of healthy narcissism. Before you can be in a relationship, you need to know how to care for yourself in a healthy way.

Setting Boundaries Helps To Clear Clutter In Your Life

Your thinking will become clearer and more focused, eliminating a lot of mental clutter. This will help you to begin clutter clearing projects.

Happily, your habit of picking up after others, pleasing them, and feeling responsible for their feelings, including tolerating misuse of your space and possessions, will go away.

Learning to set boundaries affords you a way to let go of old ways of thinking and acting that have kept you from the life you desire.

Many people grew up in homes that emphasized thinking of others' needs before their own. Parents sometimes told their children they should be liked by everyone and that other people's bad behavior needed to be tolerated in order to be liked and accepted. This pattern of thinking led to your allowing others to take advantage of you. Over time this can develop into loose and poorly defined limits which are often irritating to others around you. For instance, if you are terribly hot and sweaty and there is a fan in the room, you don't ask to have it turned on because you don't put a priority on your own comfort, and instead worry what others will think. It's better to state what would make you more comfortable, yet you don't do it because of your fears and lack of awareness. You have not defined the limits of your own lack of comfort, so you cannot speak up for your basic needs.

THE FOLLOWING FEARS TEND TO PARALYZE PEOPLE WITH POOR BOUNDARIES

- Fear of hurting others' feelings
- Fear of abandonment and separateness

- Fear of someone else's anger
- Fear of punishment
- Fear of being shamed
- Fear of being viewed as selfish
- Fear of being unspiritual
- Fear of an overcritical conscience
- Fear of loneliness
- Fear of always needing approval
- Fear of feeling guilty

When you set out to create healthy boundaries, many, if not all, of your fears will disappear.

PEOPLE WHO HAVE SOFT OR UNSURE BOUNDARIES OFTEN SAY THE FOLLOWING:

1. I can't make up my mind.

2. I have difficulty saying "no."

3. I am a people pleaser.

4. People take or use my things without asking.

5. I find it hard to express what I really want, like, or want to do.

6. I spend so much time helping others that I neglect my own needs and/or desires.

7. I have a hard time knowing what I really feel.

8. Decisions are hard for me to make.

9. I feel responsible for others' feelings.

How Can I Set Healthy Boundaries?

Step One: Recognize Boundary Issues

Boundaries emerge from what we believe we deserve and don't deserve. This is intertwined with self-esteem. Some people don't recognize that something is bothering them, or hurting them, or making them angry. They suppress their feelings and constantly feel that everything is their fault. They don't bring up their needs and feelings and stay busy enough to ignore and suppress them. Feelings of anger and rage, complaining, and whining are clues that boundaries need to be set. Feeling uncomfortable, suffocated, overlooked, and not considered around certain people are also signs that boundaries have been violated.

You may be ignoring the knot in the pit of your stomach, the headache, the cramp in the neck, the stiffness in your shoulders, or the sadness that occurs when people invade your space and take away your time and energy. The next time this occurs don't reach for the Excedrin, Zantac, or Tums, instead consider whether it is a physical reaction to a boundary violation.

Step Two: Set Necessary Boundaries

Journaling can record your feelings and help you think more clearly after your boundaries have been trampled and your feelings hurt. Writing creates clarity. Ask yourself if this is a constant pattern with this person. You can practice what to say, remaining calm. Be clear and firm, and use as few words as possible. When talking with someone about your boundaries, don't be defensive, and avoid justifying, rationalizing, or apologizing. Speak up clearly and kindly, yet decisively, to assert your wishes. If you are still angry, a letter is a good way to clear the air.

Trying to fix someone else's upset feelings does not set workable boundaries with them. You are not responsible for others' feelings, just as others are not responsible for yours. Setting your own boundaries firmly and clearly will give you a strong center and enable you to avoid getting involved with other peoples' upsets. Be very careful of forming triangles with others.

Step Three: Enforce Boundaries

It does no good to set boundaries unless you are willing and absolutely ready to enforce them. People generally have a sixth sense and know when you have reached your limit, yet that is not enough. Knowing your limits and clearly letting others know will change your relationships at work and at home.

You will be tested when you start to set boundaries and change the way you relate to situations. Plan on being tested big time. Stay calm. You may experience some loss (friendships, job, anger from family members) in the process, but you will gain more.

Be confident and go about your business with your new way of handling yourself. It will be a surprise to others who may not know how to handle the new demands that you are placing on the relationship. Stick to your goals and their protests will diminish and eventually disappear.

Try to match your behavior with the boundaries that you have set. If you have stated a limit about not receiving phone calls after a certain hour and a household member answers and brings you the phone, restate your rule and stick to it; don't take the call. In this way, family and friends will be reminded of your desires and respect your boundaries more and more.

Do not allow toxic and negative people to enter your life, home, or workspace.

Be careful, because old habits may pull you away from your focus on setting clear boundaries and asking for what you want. Users (people who tend to use others) may get angry because they can no longer use you. It forces them to take more responsibility and they don't want to change their habits. Others, who have simply been unaware of your needs and boundaries because you weren't sharing them, may be perfectly happy to comply.

Things To Think About

1. Setting limits protects your primal need for safety and security.

2. Respect others' limits without withdrawing emotionally.

3. Develop the ability to be emotionally attached to others without giving up your sense of self.

4. People who set effective limits exhibit self-control and show responsibility and respect for themselves, creating mutual balance.

5. Boundaries protect your external space, which preserves your internal space and feelings.

6. Take ownership and responsibility for your own needs by establishing and stating your boundaries.

7. People who tend to control or use others have little respect for boundaries.

8. Time is a boundary, too. What are your habits around project deadlines, holidays, luncheons, appointments, meetings, and volunteering? Do you use your time well?

9. The person with out of control time boundaries inconveniences others, minimizes their distress, rationalizes their lateness, and also often neglects to plan ahead.

10. Skin is a boundary. You may react when someone comes too close for comfort.

CHAPTER 14

Take Charge of Your Clutter

✿ QUIZ

1. **Do you fear tax time?**

2. **Do you fear having to extricate an important document?**

3. **Do you get headaches, stiff necks, back tension, or grind your teeth because your mess is always on your mind?**

Looking around your home or office, what do you see? Are piles of papers on your desk, dining room table, counters, and shelves taking up space in your life? You face this scene every day and it does not rest easily on your mind. Do you also feel this way about the messes in corners, clothes on the floor, messy and disorganized closets, and on and on? In this chapter, you will find even more new ideas and strategies for clearing your clutter.

Your Childhood Can Affect Your Present Home

Some of my students reminded me of a widespread problem. They discovered that they leave papers in piles and tolerate clutter because as children they kept their home organized and functioning due to some disability of either or both of their parents. Now, living in their own homes, they don't want reminders of that epoch of their lives. They have created their own standards for what is allowable in their environment. It appears to work for them as a way to deal with their childhood memories. The established order in their homes is "no pressure to do anything." This is in stark opposition to the way their homes were organized while they were growing up. They are not disturbed by floating papers and piles and other forms of clutter in their homes. They keep track of what's in which piles, and if the pile is disturbed, they can't find things. One student remarked that files don't work for her. She has her own system and it functions just fine for her.

Healing childhood issues enables you to create a home that supports who you want to be now or become in the future, not who you were conditioned to be earlier in your life. Living in a home that reflects unresolved issues from your childhood brings with it the possibility that these issues will continue on a subconscious level into your current life, coloring every decision and choice you make.

Denise Linn, in her book *Feng Shui for the Soul*, provides a wonderful visualization to help clear childhood issues on page 59.

CLEARING CHILDHOOD ISSUES

Close your eyes. Relax. Visualize your body shape shifting to the body you occupied as a child. Now imagine exploring your childhood home (or homes). Notice your feelings, memories, attitudes. As you continue to explore your home, ask yourself how you feel about it, if you like it, if there are any places in it that you don't like it, or any places that bring up bad memories for you.

Now imagine that you are in your present home. As you journey through your house, notice if there are any places that have the same feeling as your childhood home. If you find a negative association, then you can choose to explore and change this area.

Open your eyes and sit for a moment, reflecting on your experience.

Cleaning Your Physical Space

First, Ask Yourself These Questions

- How much of my stuff does not contribute to my comfort, efficient living, or joy?

- Do I feel overwhelmed when I look at or move around my home?

- Do I put off important decisions because they seem too difficult to focus on?

- Have I stopped entertaining because I am embarrassed about my home?

- Do I yearn to escape, burn it all, or seek therapy?

- Do I desire to have more time to volunteer and contribute to my community?

Second, Do These Things to Clear Your Physical Clutter

Here are ten things you can institute in your home to create less chaos and, of course, less physical clutter as well. It is terribly important to find some way to do these because living clutter-free requires structure, rules, and boundaries that all members of the household agree to honor.

Physical clutter in your environment causes lack of focus, loss of energy, and takes your mind away from more important matters. All this adds up to lots of chaos. Your mind and body clamor for peace, order, and a space that nurtures you instead of a space that does not take care of your basic needs.

1. Take trash out every day, or at least when the basket is almost full.

2. Do all the dishes before you retire in the evening. Imagine entering a ship-shape kitchen first thing in the morning.

3. Straighten up last thing before bed so when you arise, your home is in order.

4. Don't leave clothes lying around.

5. Put all the dirty laundry in laundry baskets.

6. Make your bed in the morning.

7. Toss packaging in the garbage as soon as you unwrap the items.

8. Schedule household chores one each evening. Then you don't have to spend a whole day doing them.

9. Toss old newspapers and magazines in the recycling bin.

10. Give your children the gift of an organized and calm environment. It will teach them to value it and how to create one for themselves.

WITH EVERY DIFFICULTY YOU FACE,
ORIENT YOURSELF TO THE SOLUTION.

❧ TIP ❧

Research has shown it takes twenty-one days to change a habit. The projects listed below will give you one to do every day for twenty-one days. They are designed to be easily accomplished in about 30 minutes. Some may require several sessions.

Twenty-one Projects

Here are some suggestions to keep the momentum going:

- ❑ Review your reasons for doing these projects or for change in general.

- ❑ Create mental pictures of yourself as having already succeeded with your habit change.

- ❑ Create affirmations about your habit change, for example: I am making progress on my …

- ❑ Reward yourself in whatever way you find that feeds your resolve.

- ❑ Take one day at a time.

Do one of these each evening or break them down into smaller, more manageable projects and you will have eliminated a great deal of clutter from your life easily.

1. Give away any shoes that are not comfortable.
2. Clean your purse.
3. Clean out your wallet.
4. Clean out extra or outdated credit cards.
5. Straighten up your jewelry box.
6. Clean up your sock drawer.
7. Clean up your underwear drawer.
8. Clean up your junk drawers.
9. Clean the cabinet under your sink.
10. Clean up all emails, trash, etc., on your computer.
11. Gather all your scarves, ties, and belts and give them a proper holder in your closet.
12. Throw away your stash of old catalogs.
13. Clean up the front door of your refrigerator.
14. Clean up the inside of the refrigerator door.
15. Go through your table linens.
16. Clean up one part of the pile on your desk.
17. Clean up a selected number of files and resolve to get to the rest in an organized fashion.

18. Go over everything in the hall closet.

19. Clean out the items stored under your bed.

20. Go over your shoe, bag, and hat collections.

21. Clean up your dining room table and set it for eating
(this discourages unopened mail and odd papers from
landing there) and keep it looking spiffy.

The Gifts Of Clearing Clutter

As you begin to take charge of your clutter and make some changes you will notice that clearing the messes around you brings you
many gifts.

❑ Clearing clutter removes stagnant, sticky, icky, swamp-
like energy from your home and office, which might also
include dust, mold, and bacteria that are growing on
piles as well.

❑ Clearing clutter frees you from being bound by the past
and gets you closer to who you can and desire to be.
Clearing clutter also does away with the mind chatter
(mind clutter) that keeps you stuck, going round in
circles, and questioning your sanity.

❑ Clearing clutter eliminates the feeling of being
overwhelmed and unable to organize your thoughts that
prevents you from starting a space-clearing project.

- ☐ Clearing clutter unearths lost things such as jewelry, letters, journals, diaries, and important papers.

- ☐ Clearing clutter increases your potential for doing the things you have put off. You will discover that your energy levels go up, you see things more clearly, and you will begin letting go of negative self-talk.

- ☐ Clearing clutter gets rid of the sense of stagnation and being stuck. You will see ways to get rid of toxic and non-nurturing relationships as well as ways of having fewer arguments with family members. You will be free of habits that don't serve you or your family.

- ☐ Clearing clutter can actually help you lose weight. Living in a stuffed environment encourages you to also stuff your mouth.

Things To Think About

1. Assign each family member a separate drawer, cubbyhole, basket, or shelf for their projects, mail, arts and crafts, school papers, etc.

2. Buy a labeler and put your name on eyeglasses, backpacks, etc.

3. Attach incoming bills to a clipboard. Bring it and your checkbook to the sofa and pay bills while watching your favorite TV programs.

4. Reward yourself frequently for jobs accomplished, schedules you stuck to, and successful completion of projects.

5. Find others who will benefit from your extra items, such as local school or community drama groups or other organizations.

6. Put your vision and/or goals on an audio tape and listen to it in the car, while exercising, and/or at odd moments.

CHAPTER 15

Steps to Clean Your Clutter

> ## ✌ QUIZ
>
> 1. Do you understand the importance of rewarding yourself?
>
> 2. Are you able to allow feelings to surface when doing clutter clearing?
>
> 3. Do you understand the importance for scheduling small segments of time to do projects?

Help, I am drowning, I don't know where to start or what to do about it all."

I hear this refrain from many of my students and readers of my book, *Clean Your Clutter, Clear Your Life*. Clutter creates so much chaos, confusion, and anxiety that taking care of it baffles most people. You know clearing it means you will root around in your past and expose areas of your mental, emotional, and spiritual neglect. You must attend to it, regardless, or your life will never change or improve.

Follow the plan I have outlined in this chapter and you will see improvement immediately.

What follows are step-by-step instructions to bring about change and provide you with a plan. *Let's DO it.*

Step One

You have already done the first step. You have become acutely aware of the clutter around you and the need to do something about it. Yea for you!

Step Two

1. Look at all your stuff and evaluate whether you need it, love it, use it, or if it brings you joy. If you answered "no" to all of these questions, the object needs to go.

2. If the object holds memories and sentiments, you can still let it go, give it away, or sell it. Take a picture of it so you have a record in a scrapbook that you can revisit any time. Free yourself of care-taking the actual item.

3. Letting go of stuff that doesn't serve you any longer makes room for new things to come into your life.

Step Three

1. Decide which is the most urgent, frustrating, or irritating pile of clutter in your home or office.

2. List the other piles in order of importance. It's a good time to glance at the list with your three short-term and three long-term goals (Chapter 1) and use this as a reference point.

3. You may want to set aside some boxes for the projects you have planned. (They may be around for a while as you complete your projects.) You can label them TRASH, DONATE/CHARITY, GARAGE SALE, REPAIRS, TRANSITION/ THINK ABOUT.

Be prepared for more of a mess to develop as you clear out closets, drawers, and piles. This is only temporary and will subside as you create more order around you.

Step Four

1. Break your first project down into small segments of 15–30 minute sessions. Perhaps you only have that amount of time each day or even each week to work on your first task. That's okay. Rome wasn't built in a day. Your efforts will result in many benefits (described in previous chapters) and before you know it you will be finished.

STUFF ATTRACTS DUST.
BUGS LOVE STUFF. MOLD LOVES STUFF.

2. Remember to concentrate on what you can do in the time you have set aside, not the entire task and the amount of time to finish the entire job. Don't get tied to the task and forget about the time segment you planned. Sometimes it is best to do small increments and get the job done after several sessions. Trying to tackle the entire project and forgetting about your time allotment will add stress and complicate things.

3. Make an appointment with yourself to do the project and schedule the time

4. Write it on your calendar and keep your commitment.

5. Eliminate excuses like: "I don't have the time or I will do it later."

❧ TIP ❧
Don't add to the piles or projects that you have chosen to work on.

Step Five

Create a visualization process for doing your first project and any others that you decide to do later.

VISUALIZATION

1. Close your eyes and take three deep breaths in through your nose and out through your mouth.

2. In your mind, see the space, pile, or project you want to clear.

3. See yourself working on the project in an organized and deliberate manner.

4. Smell the lavender or vanilla scents and hear the music you have chosen.

5. Sense how easy it is do your work and how quickly it gets done.

6. See the space cleared and orderly. Your job is done.

7. Feel the sense of freedom and joy you have now.

8. Bless your space and open your eyes.

9. Say to yourself, "I feel so much better since clearing my clutter. I can now enjoy my surroundings and go forward with my life."

OTHER VISUALIZATIONS

❑ Create a vision of what you want your space to look like. Ask yourself how this setting looks and feels.

❑ Picture your space now and after you have completed your first project.

❑ In your mind, create an island of refuge in your home. Redo your bedroom so that it becomes a restful, relaxing, sensual, and romantic retreat. Do the same for your bathroom or kitchen.

❑ Picture yourself riding through your home on a magic carpet that allows you to view your possessions from above ground level. This gives you a new vantage point and perspective on your state of affairs.*

* From Michelle Passoff, *Lighten Up.*

Step Six

It is of great importance that you take care of yourself while working on your projects.

Here's a list of self-care activities to choose from as the need arises. These can be used before you start, after the cleaning session, or as breaks while you are working.

- Take a walk or go on a short hike.

- Do some deep breathing.

- Do a session of yoga, tai chi, or chi kung.

- Do an aerobics session.

- Do some gardening.

- Take a hot aromatherapy bath.

- Take an epsom salts soaking bath.

- Read something enjoyable or inspiring.

- Meditate.

- Write in your journal.

- Take five minutes to read some articles you have been saving.

- Go outside and walk in your bare feet.

- Do a few minutes of a creative project you have started.

- Buy fresh flowers for yourself as congratulations for a job well done or to spruce up the area of work

- Hang a crystal in the window to get the benefit of the beautiful rainbows.

- Turn your face to the sun.

- Make yourself a hot cup of relaxing chamomile tea.

- Write down everything that you appreciate about your life, friends, and family.

- Take a five-minute stretch.

- Give yourself a mini-massage.

- Move your jaw around to relieve pressure.

- Go around the room and clap, ring bells, or drum.

- Have a friend call you to see how you are doing and to give you support.

- Count the blessings in your life.

- Take five minutes to write down your goals.

There are many more, but you get the general idea. Start taking care of yourself when you need to and remember to treat your chosen project with respect.

As you finish your first session and those thereafter, you may notice that you feel tired, even depressed, and emotional. This is quite normal. Your cleaning and clearing have raised the dust of old feelings and thoughts, as well as the chaotic energies and feelings that have existed in the jumbled mess. Possessions, papers, and piles actually store these energies, creating a negative charge that hovers over and in all the stuff around you. The stagnating swamp-like effect they have on your space also permeates your emotional state. I guarantee your energy will return and you will feel lighter and more positive after the project is completed.

Step Seven

Start to work on your assigned project. Work for the allotted time and then stop.

Reward yourself after completing the project with a bubble bath, a manicure or pedicure, bottle of wine, special dinner or lunch, an ice cream with a friend, or a movie. Be sure to give yourself something special after each project or section of a project is completed.

As one way of rewarding and taking care of yourself say the following:*

> "I deserve...
>
> to be loved and cherished
>
> to be excited and welcomed
>
> to give to others and to share my skills
>
> to rejoice and laugh
>
> to appreciate what I have
>
> to give blessings to others"

*Source: CLUTTER! It's Not My Fault, by Maxine M. Shapiro (page 39).

↝ TIP ↜

- ❑ Release what is not of value to you or doesn't serve you anymore. Give it to someone or some organization that will make use of it and appreciate it.

- ❑ Lightening up your stuff by recycling, donating, selling or giving it away allows you to devote your time and care to the things you love and that deserve to be cherished.

Things To Think About

1. Work with the way you function. Are you an evening or a morning person?

2. If you don't have large chunks of time, grab ten minutes from here and there in your schedule.

3. Equip yourself for successfully completing your projects by gathering all the appropriate supplies needed before you start.

STUFF DOESN'T CREATE A FULFILLING LIFE; YOU DO.

The sidebars that appear in this chapter were inspired by some ideas in *The Complete Idiot's Guide to Organizing,* by Georgene Lockwood.

CHAPTER 16

Taking Care of Yourself

✒ QUIZ

1. Are you able to take care of yourself while working on your projects?

2. Are you able to schedule time for a project and stick to it?

3. Can you develop personalized visualizations for yourself to make your work go easier and faster?

Spring Clean Your Life is about transforming your spaces into supportive, harmonious, and nurturing places in which to live and work. You have learned that clutter clearing does not have to be a horrific chore that you constantly put off, but can become a transformational experience that releases negative feelings, generates more energy, and encourages you to create what you want in your life. You now understand why clutter drains your energy, prevents you from achieving your goals, blocks your ability to think clearly, affects your health, and even limits your relationships and opportunities. You now see the ways that mental, emotional, and spiritual clutter are interconnected and, along with physical clutter, influence your life, thinking, and behaviors.

It is so important to maintain a positive attitude while clutter clearing or even when just thinking about it. Laughter is good for everything. Remember that laughter can help you reduce stress.

> I emphasize taking small steps. First write down your goals. Then plan out your projects, breaking them into manageable segments. Finally, remember to reward yourself frequently. As your projects get done, you will feel a sense of renewed energy, increased positive feelings, and soaring self-esteem. In short, your sense of well-being in every area of life will grow. Clearing your clutter will clean the cobwebs from your life and create space for new ideas, goals, and aspirations that didn't have a chance to come to the surface before.

Cleaning your house is a wonderful way for you to re-energize and get some exercise at the same time. It will also make you feel you have accomplished something worthwhile. And you get a self-esteem boost!

Lighten up occasionally and have an ice cream with a friend. A half-hour of companionship and conversation is a great picker upper. It also frees you from letting food run your life, which can also be a form of clutter, believe it or not.

SOME WAYS TO TAKE CARE OF YOURSELF

1. Use visualizations such as those found in Chapter 15.

   Use written affirmations: positive, present tense, specific, and personal. Examples:

   - I am making thoughtful and planned choices from my 'to buy' list.

   - I get rid of something if I decide to buy an item.

2. Speak your desires out loud to your partners, loved ones, friends, and work buddies.

3. Act the part by beginning small, setting the stage for achievable projects, and doing the project for just 15 minutes.

4. Feed your mind with reading, viewing, and listening to upbeat and proactive ideas.

5. Associate with positive people.

6. Teach others or tell others what you have learned and achieved. Teaching is the best way to learn. You become what you teach.

You need to identify your needs and get your needs met. To accomplish that you have to:

❏ Sort out what is yours and what is not yours.

❏ Give up "all or nothing" thinking.

❏ Give up being responsible for everything, including the feelings of others.

❏ Work on your self-esteem.

❏ Stop neglecting your own needs.

❏ Learn how to handle conflict better.

❏ Learn to set boundaries about others' inappropriate behavior.

Here are some activities that will make your changes, new habits, and goals easier to attain.

These reduce stress, are quick ways to recharge your spiritual batteries, help you think more clearly, and dispel negative feelings and thinking patterns. Use these as you work on your chosen projects.

• Stretch. Take just one minute to bend, twist, and lengthen your body. This resupplies oxygen to your muscles and brain.

- Give your jaw a workout. Stress is often stored in the TMJ joint of your jaw. Chew some gum or eat an apple to aid in loosening up these tense muscles.

- Brush your teeth. The cool running water freshens your breath and your outlook.

- Take a whiff of lavender oil. Lavender is known to have a relaxing effect.

- Declutter your workspace: Create a new view of your situation with a clean sweep of the arrangement on your desk.

- Give yourself a mini-massage. Rub your neck and scalp and pull on your ears for a quick energizer.

- Turn your face to the sun. Take a quick walk outside as a break and let your face soak up the healing and rejuvenating powers of the sun.

- Go on a mental vacation. Travel in your mind to your favorite spot or create a 3–5 minute vacation somewhere you would like to go. This frees your mind for a few moments from a stressful activity so you can return to your task with a new frame of mind.

- Fix yourself a cup of relaxing tea. This is a good break to take. While sipping and holding a warm mug of chamomile tea, relax and review your efforts and successes.

- Grab a healthy snack. Fluctuating blood sugar levels can play havoc with your ability to concentrate, think clearly, focus, and be positive.

- Write down your frustrations. This is supportive and cleansing. Reviewing your list gives you a new view of what has been stressing you.

- Count your blessings. Think about your recent successes and the people you love. Focus on the positives in your life.

- Call a reassuring friend. Chatting for a few moments with someone who cares about you and knows you well can offer you the encouragement you need to get through a hard task.*

*Source: These are excerpts from an article that appeared in *Womans Day*, 11/1/03. They are from Nancy Rosenberg's book: *Outwitting Stress: A Practical Guide to Conquering Stress Before You Crack.* Don't forget the wonderful list of self-care activities on pages 123–125 designed to help you take care of yourself.

Each chapter in this book walks you through individual projects and new habits that can become tools to clear all forms of your clutter. If you apply the ideas in *Spring Clean Your Life,* you will succeed. Order and organization is not an end in itself but a way for you to function effectively and effortlessly. Clutter clearing is another way to honor, nurture, and value yourself. When people say, "take care of yourself," you will think of your space clearing projects as a positive form of self care. You will begin to turn to clutter clearing instead of popping aspirins or running for a sweet. Your friends and family will notice something different about you. You will seem energized and enthusiastic yet calm and peaceful.

FEAR=FALSE EXPECTATIONS APPEARING REAL.

Things To Think About:

1. Clutter creates stagnation and makes everything grind to a halt.

2. Experience the inner rewards from clutter clearing.

3. Create a dream folder. Insert in it clippings from magazines and newspapers that you dream about having in your home or office. You may never acquire any of these things. The collecting of your dreams takes care of your desire to own them.

4. Your possessions and your home represent who you are, where you are going, and who you wish to become.

A FRIEND OF MINE TOLD ME THAT AFTER DOING A MAJOR CLUTTER CLEARING IN HER GARAGE AND HOME SHE IS ENJOYING MORE OF HER SPACE AND FEELS THAT THIS HAS PROPELLED HER TO A NEW STAGE IN LIFE. SHE LOOKED AT THE WHOLE PROCESS AS A SPIRITUAL EVENT OF MAJOR PROPORTIONS.

RESOURCES

Groups

Clutterless Recovery Groups, Inc.

Stop Clutter From Stealing Your Life Recovery Group on AOL.

12-step approach to recovery **www.clutterers-anonymous.org.**

12-step principles to relationship and the homepage for RCA (Recovering Couples Anonymous).**www.recovering-couples.org.**

Homepage for Clutterless self-help groups **www.clutter-recovery.**

A great site for medical discussion groups about hoarding and many other topics. Operated by Mass. Genera Hospital. Can also be accessed via **www.braintalk.org.**

The Simple Living Network: **www.SimpleLiving.net**

Organizations

CLUTTERLESS
Clutterless meetings provide safe places to be heard, discussions of ways to get out of the clutter trap, and practical suggestions.

CLUTTERERS ANONYMOUS
POB 91413
Los Angeles, CA 90009-1413

Based on the principles of a 12-step program that AAA uses.

OBSESSIVE COMPULSIVE ANONYMOUS
POB 215
New Hyde Park, NY 11040
(516) 741-7401

A 12-step program for people diagnosed with OCD symptoms, including hoarding. Send SASE for an information packet.

OBSESSIVE-COMPULSIVE FOUNDATION
POB 70
Milford, CT 06460
www.ocfoundation.org
The website contains a screening test for OCD

ANXIETY DISORDERS OF AMERICA
www.adaa.org
Hosts chats and message boards

THE ANXIETY DISORDERS EDUCATION PROGRAM
OF THE NATIONAL INSTITUTES OF HEALTH
www.nimh.nig.gov
On this site search under "obsessive compulsive disorder"

OCD RESOURCE CENTER
www.ocdresource.com
Treatment and support options for OCD sufferers

NATIONAL ASSOC. OF PROFESSIONAL ORGANIZERS
1033 LaPosada St.
Austin, TX 78752
512-206-0151

THE OBSESSIVE COMPULSIVE INFORMATION CENTER,
Madison Institute of Medicine
www.miminc.org
Information on treatment for OCD

CLUTTERLESS RECOVERY GROUPS, INC.

Clutterless.org

Clutterers Anonymous.net

Organizedhome.com

Helpful Sites On The Internet

www.context.org
Voluntary Simplicity Study Groups

Messies.com
Messies Anonymous
1-800-MessAway

www.simpleliving.net
The Simple Living Network

comneuro-mancer.mgh.harvard.edu
(note there is no "www" in this address).

www.NewDream.org
Center for a New American Dream

www.ocfoundation.org
Homepage for the Obsessive-Compulsive Foundation

www.PathToFreedom.com

Magazines

Natural Home and Garden Jan/Feb 2005 "Trimming Your Waste Line".

Real Simple

Organic Style

Family Circle

Woman's Day

Page Link to *Woman's Day Magazine's* 100 Top Organizing Tips:
S14R-womansday.com 2/1/05.

BIBLIOGRAPHY

Kendall, Kathleen-Tackett, *The Well-Ordered Home,* New Harbinger Publications, Oakland, CA, 2003.

Whitfield, Charles, MD, *Boundaries,* Health Communications, Inc., Deerfield Beach Fl., 1993.

Cloud, Dr. Henry and Townsend Dr. John, *Boundaries,* Zondervan Pub. House, Grand Rapids, MI, 1992.

Hemphill, Barbara and Bedrosian Maggie, *Love It Or Leave It,* BCI Press, Rockville, M.D., 2003.

St. James, Elaine, *Living the Simple Life,* Hyperion, NY, NY, 1996

St. James, Elaine, *Simplify Your Life,* Hyperion, NY, NY, 1994

De Grote-Sorensen Barbara and Sorensen, David Allen, *Six Weeks to a Simple Lifestyle,* Augsburg Fortress Press, Minn, Mn, 1994.

De Grote Sorensen, Barbara and Sorensen, David Allen, *Tis A Gift To Be Simple,* Augsburg Fortress Press, Minneapolis, MN, 1996.

Elgin, Duane, *Voluntary Simplicity,* Wm. Morrow & C0, NY, NY, 1993.

Watson,Phd., Donna, *101 Simple Ways To Be Good To Yourself.* Energy Press, A Bard Press Book, Austin, Texas, 1993.

Buckingham, Marcus & Clifton, PhD., Donald O. *Now Discover Your Strengths,* New York Free Press, NY, NY, 2001.

Benson, M.D., Herbert & Proctor, William, *The Breakout Principle*, Scribner, NY, NY, 2003.

Burns, M.D., David D. *Ten Days to Self-Esteem*, Harper Collins, NY, NY, 1993.

Fiore, PhD., Neil, *The Now Habit*, Penguin Group USA, NY, NY, 1989.

Lagatree, Kirsten M., *Checklists For Life*, Random House, NY, NY, 2000.

Tracy, Brian, *Maxium Achievement*, Simon & Shuster, NY, NY, 1993.

Linn, Denise, *Feng Shui For The Soul*, Hay House,Carlsbad, CA, 2000.

Michelle Passoff, *Lighten Up*, Harper Collins, NY, NY, 1998.

Nancy Rosenberg, *Outwitting Stress: A Practical Guide to Conquering Stress Before You Crack*, The Lyons Press, 2003.

Georgene Lockwood, *The Complete Idiot's Guide to Organizing*, Alpha Books, 2004.

Kathryn L. Robyn, *Spiritual Housecleaning*, New Harbinger Publications, Inc., CA, 2002.

Doris Janzen, *Living More With Less*, Longacre Press, Scottsdale,AZ, 1980.

Aslett, Don, *Not For Packrats Only: How to Clean Up, Clear Out, and Live Clutter-Free Forever*, Penguin Group, NY, NY, 1991

DON'T WORK OR EXERCISE IN YOUR BEDROOM,
THIS DISTURBS THE FEELING OF CALM AND SERENITY
IN YOUR PERSONAL RETREAT AND HAVEN.

INDEX

A STUDENT OF MINE REMARKED THAT THEY HAD BEEN
BURGLARIZED AND COULDN'T TELL WHAT HAD BEEN TAKEN
BECAUSE THERE WAS SUCH A MESS AROUND BEFORE,
IT ACTUALLY LOOKED THE SAME.

"To live content with small means;

To seek elegance rather than luxury, and refinement rather than fashion;

To be worthy, not respectable, and wealthy, not rich;

To study hard, think quietly, talk gently, act frankly;

To listen to stars and birds, babes and sages, with open heart;

To bear all cheerfully; do all bravely; await occasions, hurry never—in a word, to let the spiritual, unbidden, and unconscious grow up through the common.

This is to be my symphony."

—WILLIAM ELLERY CHANNING